DORLING KINDERSLEY **DK** VISUAL DICTIONARIES

THE VISUAL
DICTIONARY *of*
BASEBALL

FIELDER'S GLOVE

Lacing holds together parts of webbing

Individual spaces for each finger

Webbing

Space for thumb

Model name

Pocket

Heel

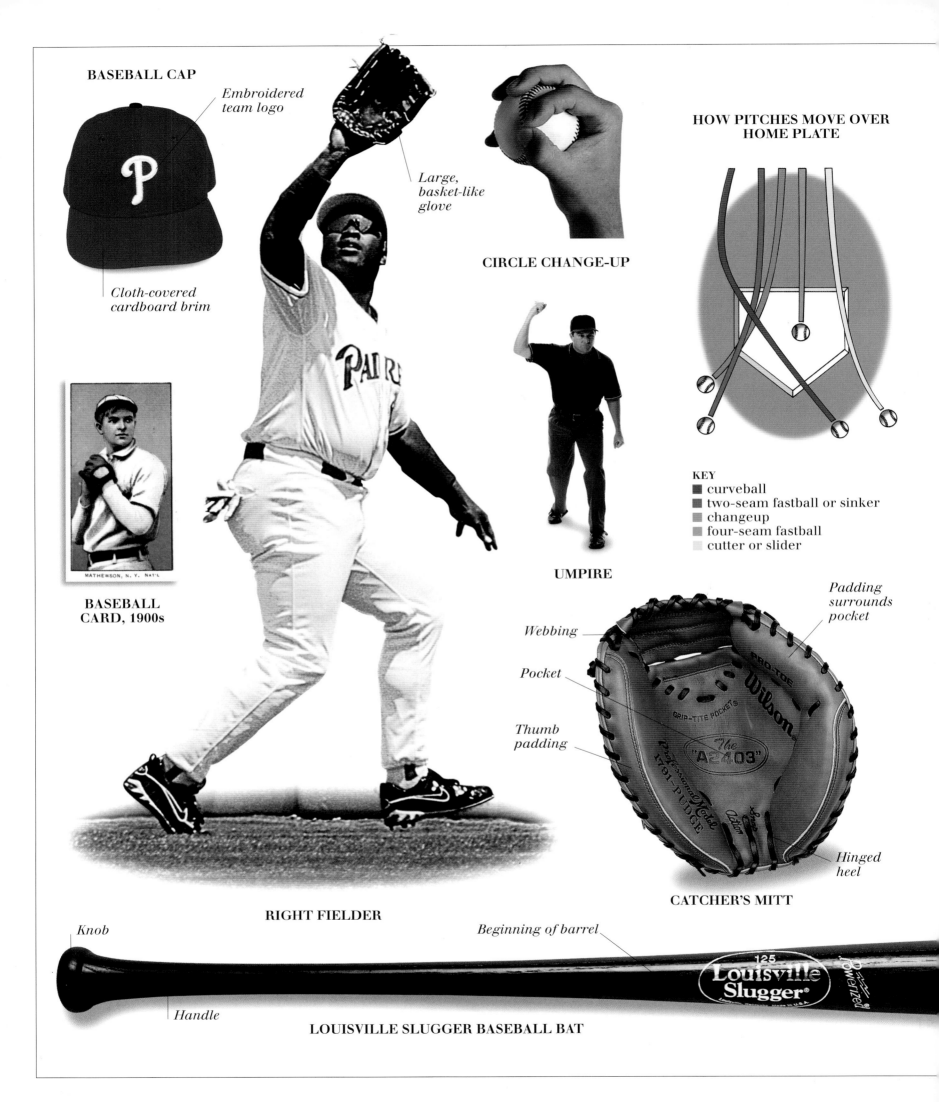

BASEBALL CAP

Embroidered team logo

Cloth-covered cardboard brim

CIRCLE CHANGE-UP

HOW PITCHES MOVE OVER HOME PLATE

Large, basket-like glove

MATHEWSON, N. Y. NAT'L

BASEBALL CARD, 1900s

KEY
- curveball
- two-seam fastball or sinker
- changeup
- four-seam fastball
- cutter or slider

UMPIRE

RIGHT FIELDER

Padding surrounds pocket

Webbing

Pocket

Thumb padding

GRIP-TITE POCKET

Wilson

PRO-TOE

"The "A2403"

Professional Model
1791-PUDGE

Hinged heel

CATCHER'S MITT

Knob

Beginning of barrel

Handle

125 Louisville Slugger® Powerized

LOUISVILLE SLUGGER BASEBALL BAT

DORLING KINDERSLEY DK VISUAL DICTIONARIES

THE VISUAL DICTIONARY *of*

BASEBALL

Written by
JAMES BUCKLEY, JR.

Chest protector

Catcher's mask

Catcher's mitt

Kneeling position
makes it hard for
runners to score

Baserunner wears
protective helmet

Shin guard

BLOCKING HOME PLATE

Sweet spot:
the best place
to hit the ball

GENUINE   C271

SEATTLE MARINERS

A Dorling Kindersley Book

Dorling **DK** Kindersley

LONDON, NEW YORK, AUKLAND, DELHI, JOHANNESBURG,
MUNICH, PARIS, SYDNEY and TORONTO

Project Editor Beth Adelman
Publisher Sean Moore
Editorial Director LaVonne Carlson

Produced by
Shoreline Publishing Group
Santa Barbara, California
Editorial Director James Buckley, Jr.
Designer Tom Carling, Carling Design, Inc.

Produced in partnership and licensed by
Major League Baseball Properties, Inc.
Executive Vice President Timothy J. Brosnan
Director of Publishing and MLB Photos Don Hintze
Major League Baseball Properties, Inc.
245 Park Avenue
New York, NY 10167

First American Edition, 2001
2 4 6 8 10 9 7 5 3

Published in the United States by
Dorling Kindersley Publishing, Inc.
375 Hudson Street
New York, New York 10014

Dorling Kindersley Publishing, Inc. offers special discounts for bulk purchases for sales
promotions or premiums. Specific, large-quantity needs can be met with special editions,
including personalized covers, excerpts of existing guides, and corporate imprints.
For more information, contact Special Markets Department,
Dorling Kindersley Publishing, Inc., 375 Hudson Street, New York, NY 10014
Fax: 800-600-9098.

Library of Congress Cataloging-in-Publication Data

Buckley, James, Jr.
    The visual dictionary of baseball / written by James Buckley, Jr. —
1st American ed.
        p.cm.
Includes index
ISBN-13: 978-0-7894-6725-6 (alk. paper)
ISBN-10: 0-7894-6725-9 (alk. paper)
    1. Baseball—Terminology. 2. Baseball—Pictorial works.
    3. Picture dictionaries, English. I. Title

GV862.3 B852001
796.357'03—dc21

00-051833

Color reproduction by Colourscan, Singapore
Printed and bound in Spain by Artes Graficas Toledo, S.A.U.

see our complete
catalog at
www.dk.com

Tiny webbing

Eyes lock in on target

Contents

Back foot drives off rubber

HERE'S THE PITCH

1920S BASEBALL GLOVE

See-through webbing aids vision

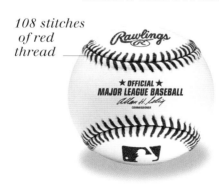

108 stitches of red thread

BASEBALL

FIRST BASEMAN

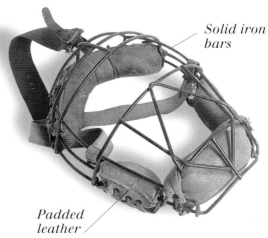

Solid iron bars

Padded leather

EARLY CATCHER'S MASK

CATCHER'S HELMET

Origins of the game

LIKE MANY IMPORTANT INNOVATIONS, baseball is the product of many parents. The game in America grew out of several centuries-old ball-and-bat games, such as rounders and town ball, that had been transplanted from England. In 1845, New York City's Knickerbocker Base Ball Club codified rules for what was first called "base ball." A game that year in Hoboken, New Jersey, is recognized as the first real baseball game. (A long-debated myth that Union Army General Abner Doubleday invented baseball in 1839 has long since been debunked.) The Knickerbocker Club helped spread the game among sportsmen in the Northeast, and the Civil War helped spread the game around the country. By the 1880s, baseball had a firm hold on the national psyche and was on its way to becoming America's National Pastime.

EARLY BAT
Baseball bats have always been round, but the early bats did not taper as much in the handle. Many were handmade and had a more rough-hewn quality than today's factory-made models.

A KIDS' GAME
This 1834 engraving shows children playing a game with ball and bat on Boston Common. Elements of baseball can be seen in the pitcher throwing to a batter, with several players in the field playing defense. Similar games in England and America contributed to the birth of baseball.

The "base paths" were pedestrian walkways in the park

Roughly formed knob

Pitcher throws ball to batter

EARLY BASEBALL
Thick leather, rough construction, and a tendency to get mushy marked early balls.

Rough hand stitching

Two-piece leather cover, similar to today's version

The re-creation featured period costumes, including a top hat

A stick at the center of the field was "home base"

Player tries to throw ball at runner

TOWN BALL
This modern re-creation shows how the baseball antecedent, town ball, was played. Batting was part of the game, but not pitching, and runners were put out by being struck, rather than tagged, by a thrown ball.

Cartwright later became a fire chief in Honolulu

ALEXANDER CARTWRIGHT
As a director of the Knickerbocker Club, Cartwright was a key figure in laying out the first rules of the game, designing the first fields with 90-foot basepaths, and organizing the first teams in the late 1840s.

Early uniforms featured collars

Boston Red Stockings of the National Association

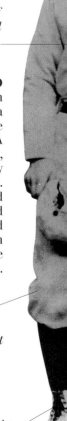

GOING PRO
As baseball grew in popularity, a professional league became inevitable. A class of sportsmen, represented here by ace pitcher Albert G. Spalding, formed pro teams and leagues, and turned baseball from pastoral pastime into big business.

Spalding later founded a sporting goods company that is still in business

High topped shoes worn for photo only

Bats or sticks were used in several ball games

The diamond

A BASEBALL DIAMOND IS NOT diamond-shaped. Rather, the field perhaps best resembles a piece of pie with an often-irregular outer edge. The infield area describes a perfect square, 90 feet on each side, between each of the four bases. However, viewed from behind home plate, the square stands on one corner and does resemble a diamond. This 90-foot-square infield, a mix of grass and dirt, is the key to the baseball diamond. A foot more or less and the timing of the entire game would be off, giving either defense or offense an advantage. This key distance became the standard in the 1860s and has remained fixed ever since. Beyond the infield is a spacious grass outfield whose boundaries vary from ballpark to ballpark. Every outfield ends with a padded wall, but the height of that wall also varies.

Outfield wall, usually padded

Outfield

Left field foul line

Typically, it's 330 to 350 feet from home plate to the outfield wall

Second base

Pitching rubber measures 24 inches by six inches

Third base

Pitcher's mound

Mound is 18 feet in diameter, raised 10 inches above the level of the field

Infield

127 feet, 3⅜ inches from home plate to second base

Batter's box

Home plate

Catcher's and umpire's box

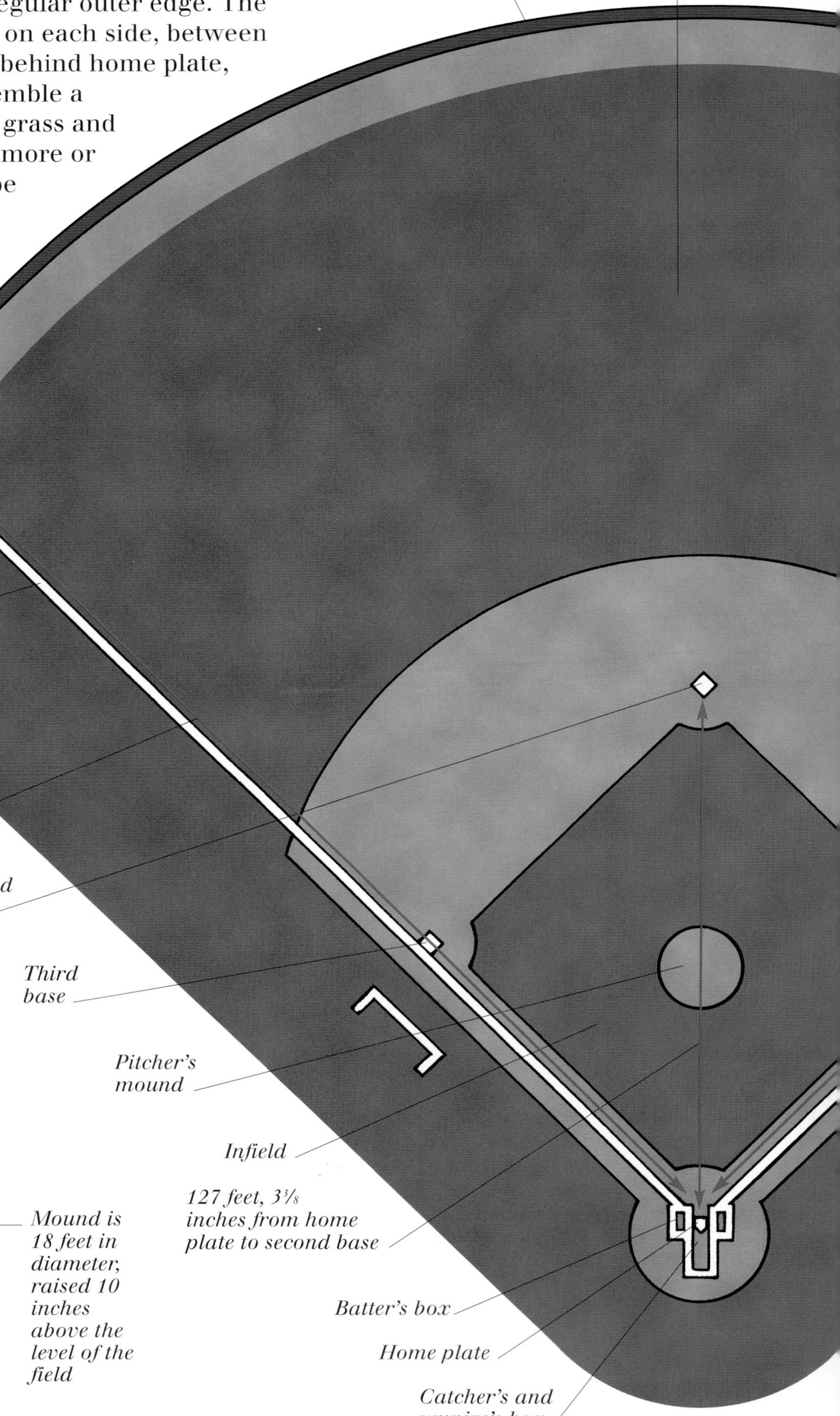

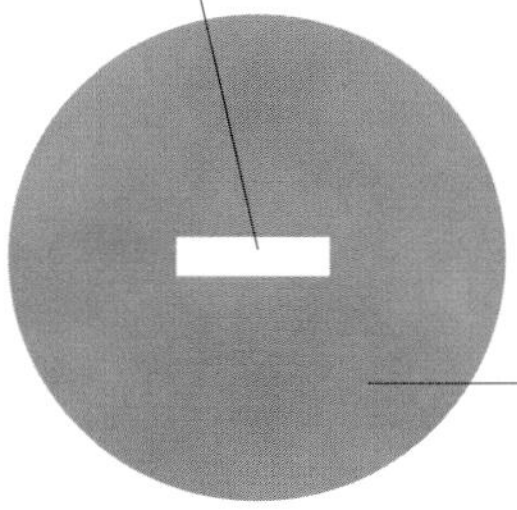

THE PITCHER'S MOUND

At the center of the diamond is a raised mound of dirt from which the pitcher throws the ball. On the mound is the pitching rubber; one of the pitcher's feet must touch the rubber to begin each pitch. Since 1893, the mound has been 60 feet, six inches from home plate.

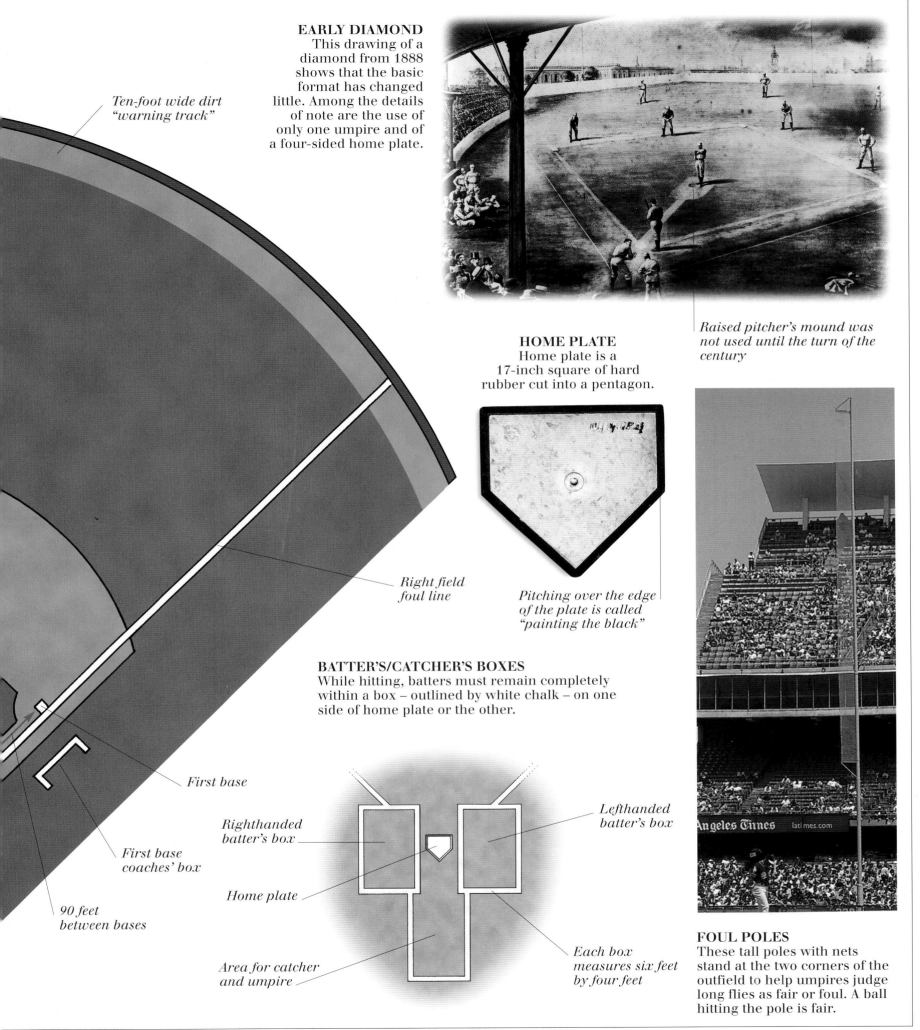

EARLY DIAMOND
This drawing of a diamond from 1888 shows that the basic format has changed little. Among the details of note are the use of only one umpire and of a four-sided home plate.

Ten-foot wide dirt "warning track"

Raised pitcher's mound was not used until the turn of the century

HOME PLATE
Home plate is a 17-inch square of hard rubber cut into a pentagon.

Right field foul line

Pitching over the edge of the plate is called "painting the black"

BATTER'S/CATCHER'S BOXES
While hitting, batters must remain completely within a box – outlined by white chalk – on one side of home plate or the other.

First base

Righthanded batter's box

Lefthanded batter's box

First base coaches' box

Home plate

90 feet between bases

Area for catcher and umpire

Each box measures six feet by four feet

FOUL POLES
These tall poles with nets stand at the two corners of the outfield to help umpires judge long flies as fair or foul. A ball hitting the pole is fair.

The rules

TWO TEAMS OF NINE PLAYERS compete over nine innings to score runs. The team with the most runs after nine innings wins the game. Each inning is made up of three outs per team; outs are recorded by the defensive team against the offensive team, who is "at bat." The basics of play: A pitcher throws the baseball toward the batter. The pitcher wants the batter to swing and miss the ball, or to hit it to one of the pitcher's teammates on the field. The batter wants to hit the ball so that he can advance safely to the bases. His ultimate goal is touch all four bases, the final one being home plate, where he will score a run for his team. That, simply stated, is baseball; but from that simplicity comes one of the world's most elegant games.

THE STRIKE ZONE

A pitch that crosses above the plate and between the batter's armpits and the top of his knees is called a strike. Three strikes are an out. Pitches outside the strike zone are called balls; four balls earn the batter a walk – a trip to first base.

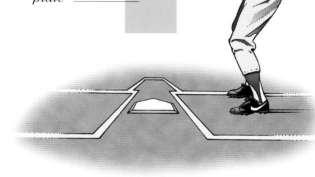

Strike zone is 17 inches wide – same as home plate

Baserunners must keep batting helmets on

A STRIKE

A batter who swings at and misses a pitch receives a strike, as demonstrated here by the great Babe Ruth. The catcher must cleanly handle any third strike; if he doesn't, the runner may try to reach first base before being tagged or forced out.

Catcher keeps ball securely in mitt while trying to make tag

SCORING A RUN

Each time a runner touches home plate without being tagged or forced out, a run is scored for the runner's team. Close plays at home plate, such as this one in which the runner scored, are among the most exciting in baseball.

Foot or any part of the runner's body must touch home plate to score a run

Catcher may block home plate with his body or legs

Ball in glove

Batter is now the baserunner

FORCE PLAY
A force play records an out when the defensive player touches the base while holding the ball, before the runner touches the base. Here, the first baseman has just received the throw from an infielder for an out, beating the runner by a fraction of a second.

Players try to avoid stepping on one another's feet at first base

FLY BALL OUTS
A batted ball that is caught before it hits the ground is an out. These can be called fly balls, pop-ups, or foul pops, depending on their height and position.

Flip-down sunglasses to battle glare

TAG OUT
If a baserunner is tagged, or touched, with the ball – or, more often, with the fielder's mitt with the ball inside it – before reaching the base, he is out. Players may slide to reach base more quickly, or in an attempt to avoid a tag.

LINE SCORE
Each of the nine innings of a baseball game has a "top" and a "bottom." The home team bats in the bottom of the inning. If the home team is ahead after the top of the ninth inning, the game is over and the bottom of the ninth is not played (as in the X, below).

R, H, E for totals of runs, hits, and errors in the game

Total runs scored in each half of the inning

Inning number

	1	2	3	4	5	6	7	8	9	R	H	E
NEW YORK	0	0	0	3	1	0	0	0	1	5	9	1
BOSTON	0	0	2	0	1	0	1	2	X	6	12	2

Bats and balls

BATS AND BASEBALLS REMAIN THE ESSENTIAL EQUIPMENT of the game. In baseball's 150 years of existence, many things about the sport have changed dramatically. From player salaries to international popularity to massive stadiums, baseball is played in a different world than when it was first invented. But the baseball and the bat remain remarkably the same, in both form and function. Technology certainly has improved their quality. For instance, mass production techniques mean Major Leaguers don't have to use one ball for an entire game, as was often the case in the 1800s. Bats are engineered to put the most wood mass possible at the bat's "sweet spot." The specifics for this equipment are easy to relate: Major League baseballs must weigh between 5 and 5 1/4 ounces, with a diameter of between 9 and 9 1/4 inches. Bats may not be more than 2 3/4 inches in diameter at the thickest point nor longer than 42 inches. But the cracking sound of wooden bat meeting leather ball means so much more than numbers. That distinctive sound is the game's soul.

AUTOGRAPHS
Baseballs are the tradtional place to get autographs of famous players, such as Babe Ruth, who signed this ball in 1948.

BASEBALLS: INSIDE AND OUT
Major League baseballs are made by the Rawlings Sporting Goods Company of St. Louis. At its factory in Costa Rica, Rawlings turns out 2 million baseballs a year for every level of baseball play. Around a cork-and-rubber central core or "pill," more than 1,300 feet of wool thread and yarn are machine-wound. For Major League balls, workers hand sew two-piece leather covers, finishing about 30 baseballs per day per worker.

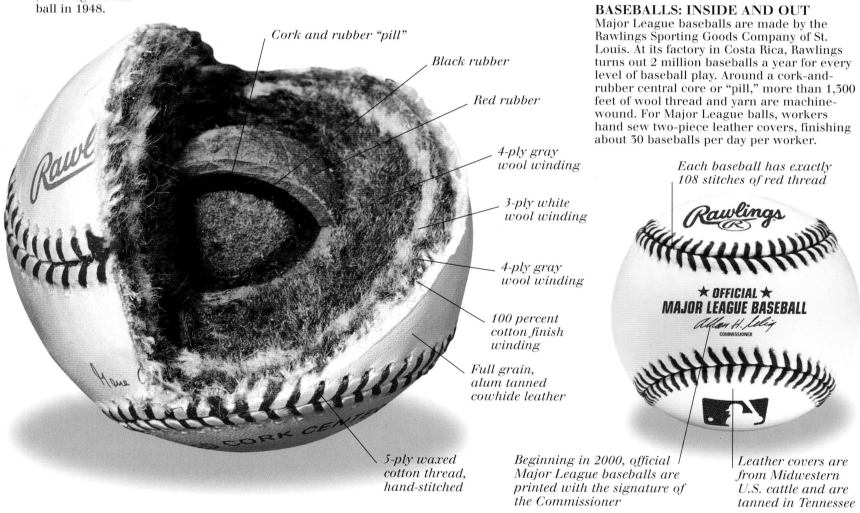

Cork and rubber "pill"

Black rubber

Red rubber

4-ply gray wool winding

3-ply white wool winding

4-ply gray wool winding

100 percent cotton finish winding

Full grain, alum tanned cowhide leather

5-ply waxed cotton thread, hand-stitched

Each baseball has exactly 108 stitches of red thread

★ OFFICIAL ★ MAJOR LEAGUE BASEBALL
Allan H. Selig
COMMISSIONER

Beginning in 2000, official Major League baseballs are printed with the signature of the Commissioner

Leather covers are from Midwestern U.S. cattle and are tanned in Tennessee

FINISHED PRODUCT
After a final sanding, the bats receive a black or dark brown laquer coating. Pro players order several dozen bats before each season, and can order more if the bats break, which most wooden bats do eventually. Many players receive their bats free in promotional arrangements with bat manufacturers. But all players still care for their bats carefully; they are the tools of their trade.

Knob

Handle

Beginning of barrel

RECORD-SETTERS

Bats and balls that have been used at important moments in baseball history or by star players to set records become valuable pieces of memorabilia, such as this equipment used by Babe Ruth and Roger Maris to set single-season home run records. Ruth hit 60 in 1927, Maris 61 in 1961; both players were with the New York Yankees.

Ball Maris hit for 61st home run

Bat used by Maris to hit 61st home run

Bat used by Ruth to hit 60th hom run

Ruth's 60th home run ball

Ruth's 42-ounce bat was about 10 ounces heavier than most modern bats.

STAGES OF CREATION

These are the steps that the Hillerich & Bradsby Company of Louisville, Kentucky, goes through to create the Louisville Slugger, the most famous model of baseball bat. A section of a tree trunk is split into sections, from which the "square" is cut. That square is then turned on a lathe sequentially to create the bat. Craftsmen making bats for Major League players do so to each player's preferences, which are on file with the company.

Knobs to hold bat in place on lathe

Ash tree bark still attached on split

Wood is from northern white ash trees at least 60 years old

After rough shape of bat is made, bat is sanded, trimmed, and made ready for laquer treatment

SPLIT   SQUARE   ROUND   ROUGH OUT   SEMI-FINISHED

Signature, name, and model number of bat for Ken Griffey, Jr. burned into the wood and painted silver

Sweet spot: the best place to hit the ball

Manufacturer's logo

Baseball gloves

EACH FIELDER WEARS A LARGE leather glove on his non-throwing hand. Different positions use different types of gloves, but all gloves are basically an extension of the hand with a basket or web between the thumb and forefinger. Baseball gloves have evolved considerably over the years, changing more than any other piece of equipment in the game. The first gloves were designed only to protect the palms and not extend the reach at all. Catchers were the first players to wear gloves that covered the whole hand, and it was not until the 1880s that all players began wearing small gloves. Over time, gloves grew longer and sleeker and the basket grew larger and deeper, extending the players' reach considerably. Today there are limits on how big gloves can be: 12 inches long and 7 ¾ inches wide in the Major Leagues, for example. As with any piece of baseball equipment, though, it is not the glove itself that is special, but what the fielders can accomplish with it.

GOLD GLOVE
The best fielders at each position in the American and National Leagues each receive the Rawlings Gold Glove award for fielding excellence. This trophy was awarded to Willie Mays in 1962. Great fielders are sometimes called simply "glove men."

Mays won 12 Gold Gloves in his 22-year Hall of Fame career

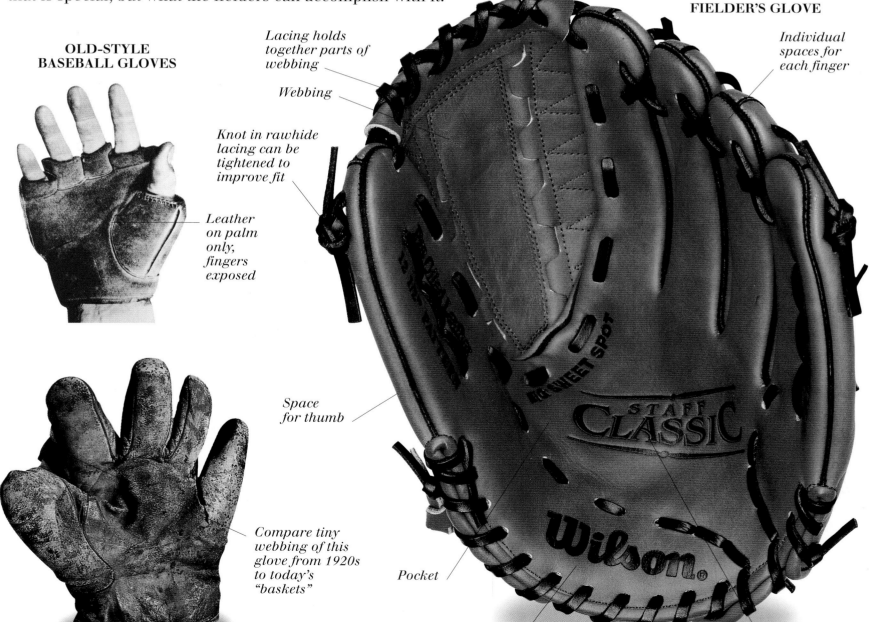

OLD-STYLE BASEBALL GLOVES

Lacing holds together parts of webbing

Webbing

Knot in rawhide lacing can be tightened to improve fit

Leather on palm only, fingers exposed

Space for thumb

Compare tiny webbing of this glove from 1920s to today's "baskets"

FIELDER'S GLOVE

Individual spaces for each finger

Pocket

Heel

Model name

PITCHER'S GLOVE

Fingers laced tightly together

Webbing made of several pieces lets glove give when catching

BATTING GLOVE

Leather fingers

Nylon back

Velcro wrist closure

See-through webbing aids vision

Deep pocket to absorb repeated hard throws

Plastic dial turns to tighten fit around wrist

Unique design lets the index finger remain out of the main part of the glove; more traditional than functional

FIRST BASEMAN'S GLOVE

Open webbing to see ball better

Longer thumb sleeve to extend reach

Flat piece of leather over finger area, rather than individual finger sleeves; better for scooping low throws

FIRST BASEMAN'S GLOVE IN ACTION
This glove is the longest and deepest. This helps first basemen stretch for high throws or scoop low throws out of the dirt.

15

Uniforms

THE TRADITIONAL BASEBALL UNIFORM consists of a jersey top, an undershirt with colored sleeves, pants whose length can fall anywhere from knee to ankle, colored stirrup socks, leather spiked shoes, and a baseball cap. While many things have changed over the years in baseball, the traditional design baseball has maintained has made its uniforms instantly recognizable for more than a century. Harry Wright of the 1869 Cincinnati Red Stockings is often credited with popularizing the knee-length pants style that was baseball's distinctive look until recent years. Wright wanted to show off the team's namesake socks. Early uniforms were made of baggy wool and got heavier as players sweated, and often players had to make do with one or two uniforms for a whole season. Today's players enjoy the benefits of modern, lightweight, stretchable, breathable materials. Teams try to use uniforms for many games, but replacements are much more readily available than in earlier times.

Embroidered team logo

BASEBALL CAP
Never called a hat, the baseball cap is made of six triangular panels held at the top by a galvanized steel button.

Cloth-covered cardboard brim

Hard plastic exterior

BATTING HELMET
Mandatory since 1969, helmets are worn by batters and baserunners for protection from the ball.

Ear hole for ventilation

Interior padding

BASEBALL UNIFORMS OVER TIME
Baseball uniform styles have changed little over the years, with materials and length of the pants being the major changes.

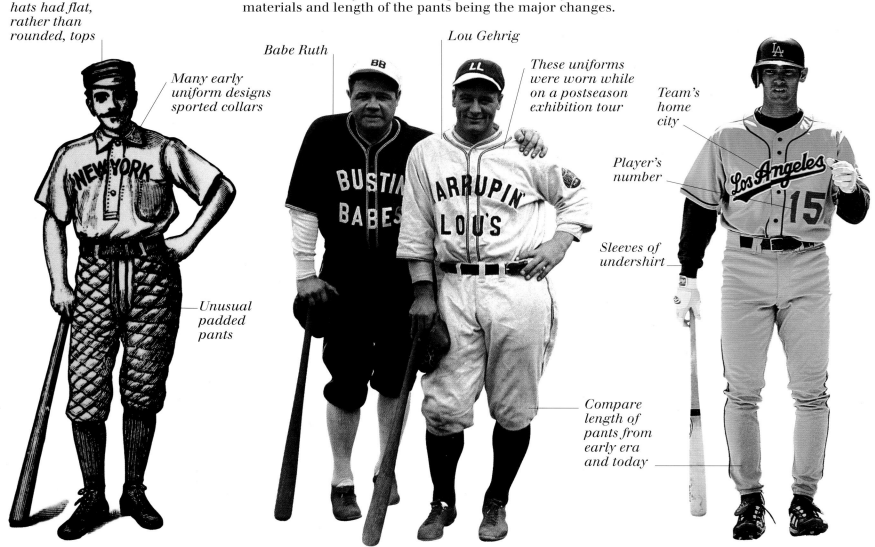

Some early hats had flat, rather than rounded, tops

Many early uniform designs sported collars

Babe Ruth

Lou Gehrig

These uniforms were worn while on a postseason exhibition tour

Team's home city

Player's number

Sleeves of undershirt

Unusual padded pants

Compare length of pants from early era and today

CIRCA 1880

1927

2000

BASEBALL UNIFORM

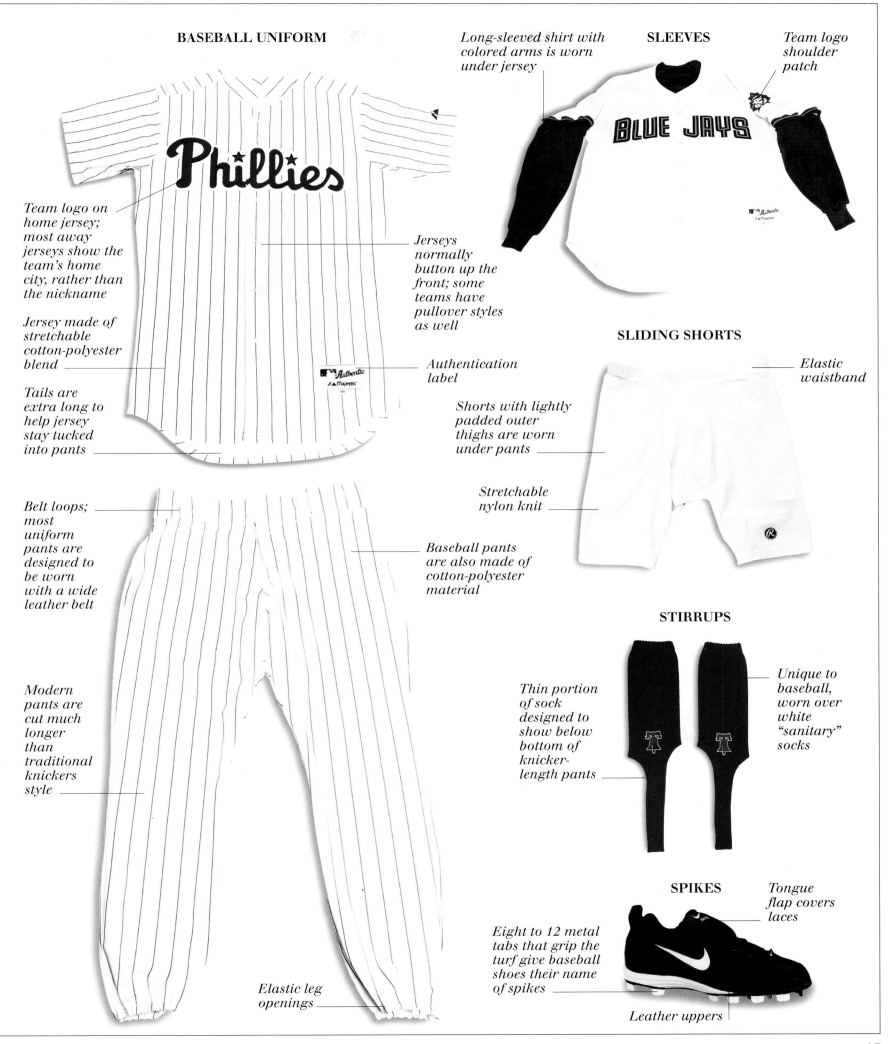

Team logo on home jersey; most away jerseys show the team's home city, rather than the nickname

Jersey made of stretchable cotton-polyester blend

Tails are extra long to help jersey stay tucked into pants

Belt loops; most uniform pants are designed to be worn with a wide leather belt

Modern pants are cut much longer than traditional knickers style

Elastic leg openings

Jerseys normally button up the front; some teams have pullover styles as well

Authentication label

Baseball pants are also made of cotton-polyester material

SLEEVES

Long-sleeved shirt with colored arms is worn under jersey

Team logo shoulder patch

BLUE JAYS

SLIDING SHORTS

Elastic waistband

Shorts with lightly padded outer thighs are worn under pants

Stretchable nylon knit

STIRRUPS

Thin portion of sock designed to show below bottom of knicker-length pants

Unique to baseball, worn over white "sanitary" socks

SPIKES

Tongue flap covers laces

Eight to 12 metal tabs that grip the turf give baseball shoes their name of spikes

Leather uppers

17

Catchers' gear

Before helmets, catchers wore their caps backward

MICKEY COCHRANE, A HALL OF FAME CATCHER, knew of what he spoke when he dubbed the gear worn by baseball catchers "the tools of ignorance." The rough-and-tumble life of a catcher – battered by baseballs, bats, and runners, and spending much of his time in an awkward crouch – makes the position suitable for only the hardiest of players. Early catchers wore no special gear at all, though they were the first players to begin wearing gloves, which grew from fingerless leather types to large, padded models to lightweight, hinged mitts. Catcher's masks were developed in the 1870s, and for a time, that was all a respectable catcher used to protect himself. In 1907, the New York Giants' Roger Bresnahan ignored the jeers of fans and became the first Major Leaguer to regularly wear shin guards; crude chest protectors had been in use for some years by then. From the tough-guy days of leather and canvas, catchers' gear has evolved with new technology, including equipment that is lighter yet stronger and more protective. The position is still difficult and dangerous, but catchers go into battle well-armed to survive to catch another day.

Old-style chest protector made of leather

Leather shin guards

Foot flap

GEAR OF YESTERYEAR
Mickey Cochrane models the gear worn by catchers in the 1930s. Without the benefit of modern high-impact plastics, catchers back then relied on heavy leather and canvas for the shin guards and chest protector.

High-impact polycarbonate cover over polypropelene lining

UNDER THE MASK
Catchers wear this brimless, padded, hard-plastic helmet beneath their masks. A helmet such as this is mandatory in youth and high school leagues.

CATCHER'S MASKS

Forehead pad; leather toward face, vinyl outside

Wider frame to protect ears

Holes for ventilation

Sturdy, lightweight hollow-wire frame

Chin and jaw pads

Throat guard

Mask covers ears

Throat guard

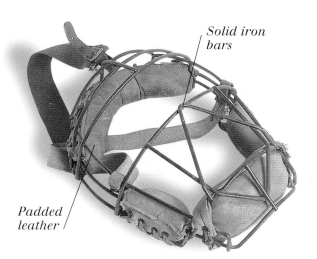

Solid iron bars

Padded leather

MODERN MASK
Most catchers today use a mask like this one, which is surprisingly similar to the earliest masks. The wide horizontal area at the center is designed to create a good view of the action. That and the other spaces in the bars are, not surprisingly, designed to keep baseballs out.

HOCKEY-STYLE MASK
A variation on the traditional mask is this one, modeled on masks used by ice hockey goalies. The cage-style bars still cover the face, but the helmet surrounds the head and sides of the neck, affording greater protection. Several pro catchers now use this style of mask.

EARLY MASK
This example from the 1920s shows how little the basic design of the catcher's mask has changed over time. Masks back then, however, were smaller and did not protect the throat.

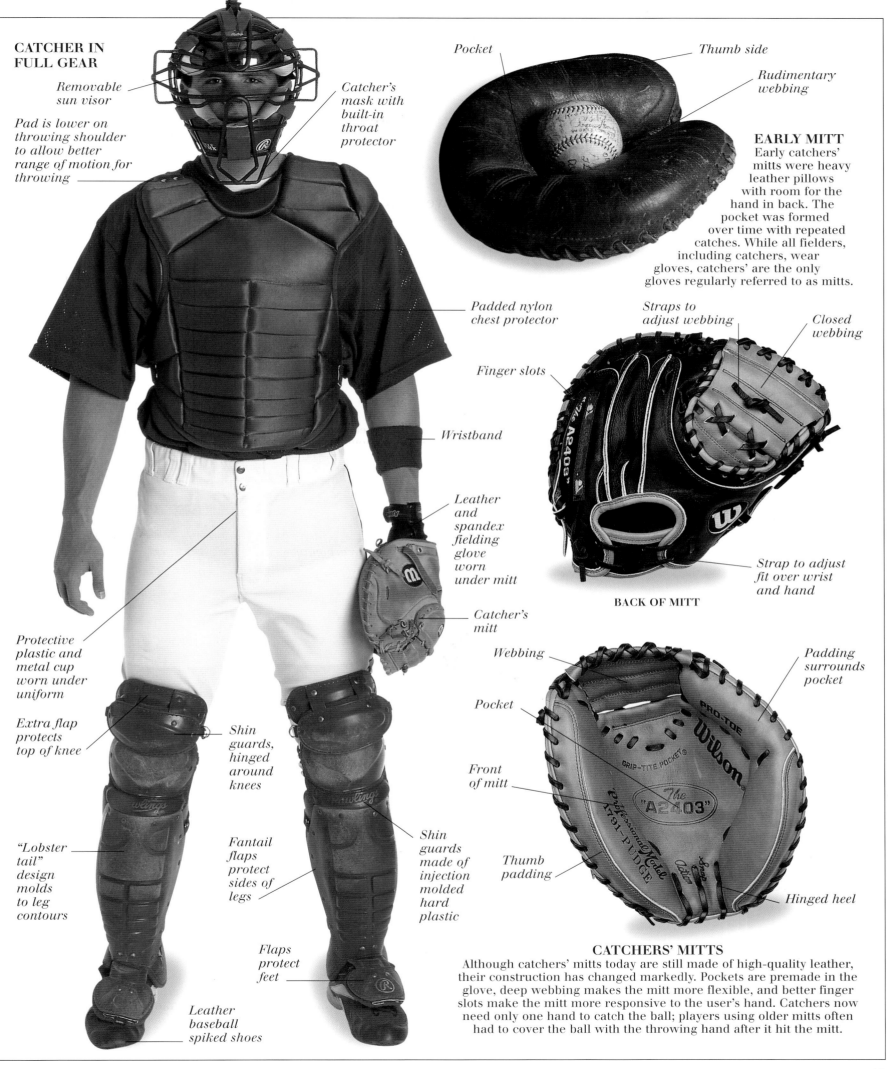

CATCHER IN FULL GEAR

Removable sun visor

Pad is lower on throwing shoulder to allow better range of motion for throwing

Catcher's mask with built-in throat protector

Padded nylon chest protector

Wristband

Leather and spandex fielding glove worn under mitt

Catcher's mitt

Protective plastic and metal cup worn under uniform

Extra flap protects top of knee

Shin guards, hinged around knees

"Lobster tail" design molds to leg contours

Fantail flaps protect sides of legs

Shin guards made of injection molded hard plastic

Flaps protect feet

Leather baseball spiked shoes

Pocket

Thumb side

Rudimentary webbing

EARLY MITT
Early catchers' mitts were heavy leather pillows with room for the hand in back. The pocket was formed over time with repeated catches. While all fielders, including catchers, wear gloves, catchers' are the only gloves regularly referred to as mitts.

Straps to adjust webbing

Closed webbing

Finger slots

Strap to adjust fit over wrist and hand

BACK OF MITT

Webbing

Padding surrounds pocket

Pocket

Front of mitt

Thumb padding

Hinged heel

PRO-TOE
Wilson
GRIP-TITE POCKET®
The "A2403"
Professional Model
K791-PUDGE
Snap Action

CATCHERS' MITTS
Although catchers' mitts today are still made of high-quality leather, their construction has changed markedly. Pockets are premade in the glove, deep webbing makes the mitt more flexible, and better finger slots make the mitt more responsive to the user's hand. Catchers now need only one hand to catch the ball; players using older mitts often had to cover the ball with the throwing hand after it hit the mitt.

Fielding positions

THERE ARE NINE POSITIONS IN a baseball team's defensive alignment, and each position is responsible for a specific area of the diamond. The division of the players into outfielders and infielders came early in baseball's history, but the number of players varied from league to league, with some sporting four outfielders. Early infielders often stood directly on the bases, and the shortstop was not created as a position until 1849 or 1850. The current alignment of four infielders, three outfielders, and the battery of pitcher and catcher was standard by the 1850s. Some physical attributes that are generally necessary for various positions include: quickness for middle infielders; strong throwing arms for third basemen; height and reach for first basemen; speed and a powerful throwing arm for outfielders (although less so for left fielders); and stamina and strength for catchers.

The key to great shortstops? It's all in the feet

SHORTSTOP
This is often called the most demanding position; he is usually a team's best defensive player.

Great reach is important when playing shortstop

Left fielder

Outfielders often use flip-down sunglasses to shield their eyes from glare on fly balls

LEFT FIELDER
Often a team's weakest fielder, he has the shortest throws to the bases. Left fielders are traditionally great hitters.

Speed to track down hits to the "alleys" is a key outfield skill

Pitchers must be constantly alert after finishing the pitch

Pitchers square their shoulders toward home plate after releasing ball

Glove is ready to snare either line drives or hard-hit ground balls

Third baseman in a ready position as the pitch is thrown

Pitcher's glove

Catchers use a quick release to get the ball to the bases

THIRD BASEMAN
Quick reactions are key to playing what is called "the hot corner." Third basemen play closest to the batter and often deal with hard-hit balls. They also have the longest infield throw to first.

PITCHER
The moment the pitcher releases the ball, he becomes another infielder and must be ready to catch ground balls or screaming line drives. Pitchers also back up infielders on throws from the outfield.

Catchers quickly plant their back foot to brace for throws to bases

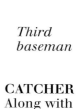

Third baseman

CATCHER
Along with receiving pitches, catchers must have strong, quick arms to throw out would-be base stealers.

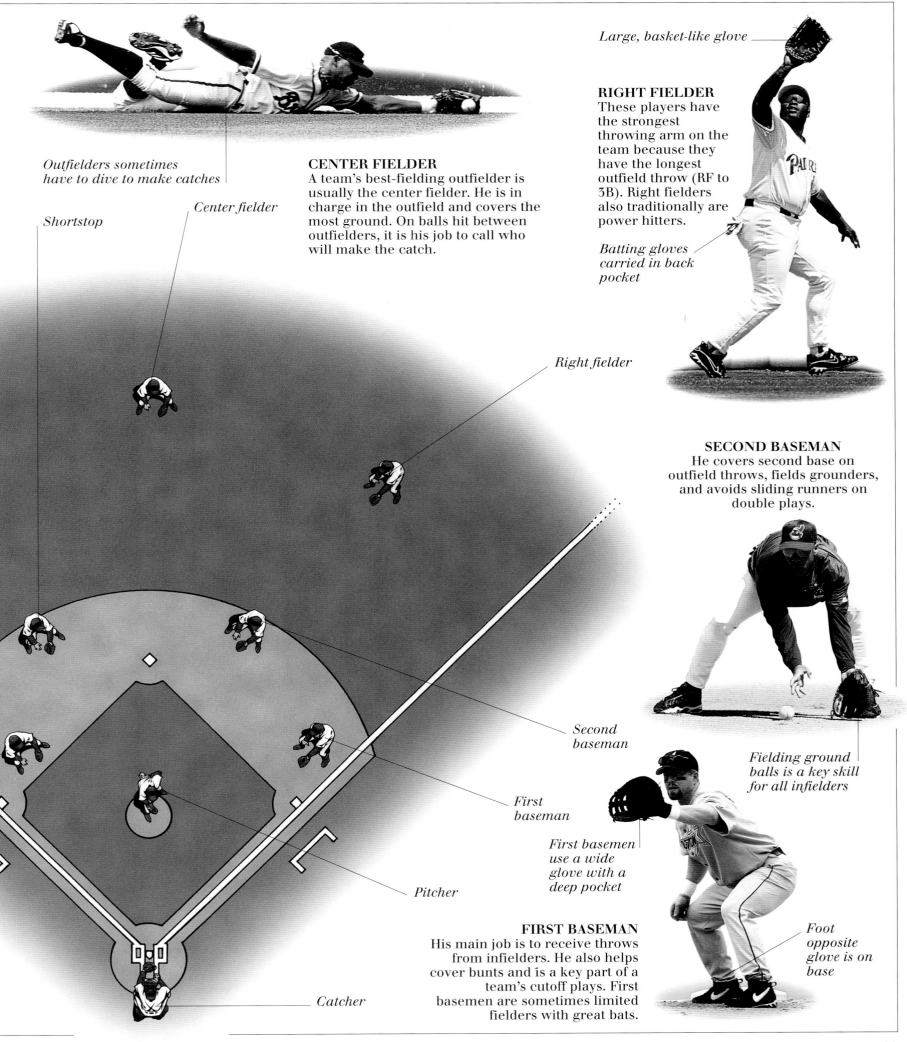

Outfielders sometimes have to dive to make catches

Shortstop

Center fielder

CENTER FIELDER
A team's best-fielding outfielder is usually the center fielder. He is in charge in the outfield and covers the most ground. On balls hit between outfielders, it is his job to call who will make the catch.

Large, basket-like glove

RIGHT FIELDER
These players have the strongest throwing arm on the team because they have the longest outfield throw (RF to 3B). Right fielders also traditionally are power hitters.

Batting gloves carried in back pocket

Right fielder

SECOND BASEMAN
He covers second base on outfield throws, fields grounders, and avoids sliding runners on double plays.

Second baseman

First baseman

Fielding ground balls is a key skill for all infielders

First basemen use a wide glove with a deep pocket

Pitcher

Foot opposite glove is on base

FIRST BASEMAN
His main job is to receive throws from infielders. He also helps cover bunts and is a key part of a team's cutoff plays. First basemen are sometimes limited fielders with great bats.

Catcher

Fielding techniques

BASEBALL'S NINE DEFENSIVE PLAYERS use a variety of skills. Each position uses specific fielding techniques, but there are three skills at which all players must excel: catching fly balls, fielding ground balls, and throwing accurately. In addition to individual skills, players work in concert with their teammates to cover the whole field. On almost any play there are a number of ways teammates back each other up. For instance, on a ground ball to the infield with no runners on base, the catcher may run to a spot behind first base in case there is an overthrow. Fielders must also always be aware of what is happening in the game: How many outs are there? Who is on base? What is the count on the batter? They keep constant track of these changing facts so that they will instantly know what to do if the ball is hit their way.

CATCHING FLY BALLS
Outfielders move to where the ball will land, and try to catch it above their heads.

Eyes watch the ball

On his toes in case wind shifts the ball

TYPICAL DOUBLE PLAY
On a double play, the defense gets two outs on one batted ball. Usually, these are on ground balls in the infield. Here, for one out the shortstop throws to the second baseman, who then throws to first to put the batter out for a double play.

Shortstop fields ball and throws to second base

Second baseman moves up to second base as ball is hit

Runner on first heads for second base when ball is hit

First baseman moves to receive throw

Batter hits ground ball to shortstop

Batter runs toward first base after hitting ball

Head tilted all the way back to follow ball

Mask is flung aside for better vision and to avoid tripping over it

KEY
- path of ball
- path of runners
- paths of fielders

FOUL POPUP
Catchers specialize in fielding high popups that are often spinning in the wind directly above their head.

Kneeling position makes it hard for runners to score

BLOCKING THE PLATE
On plays at home, the catcher makes the tag while using his body to keep the runner from touching the plate.

Catcher's mask with sun visor

RECEIVING
A catcher's main job is to receive pitches. The catcher keeps his eyes forward while giving the pitcher a good target to throw to.

Fingers pointed up to form target

Hand kept back to avoid foul tips

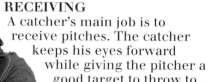

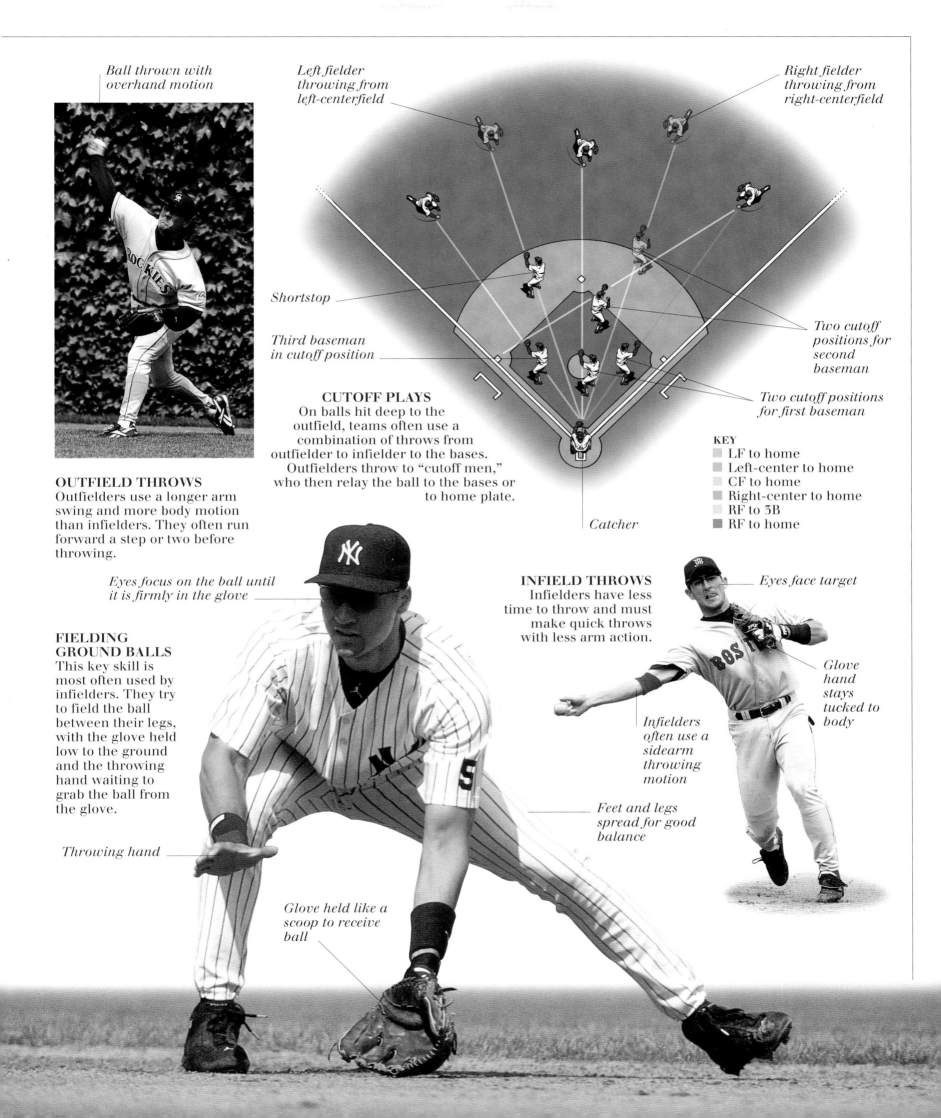

Ball thrown with overhand motion

Left fielder throwing from left-centerfield

Right fielder throwing from right-centerfield

Shortstop

Third baseman in cutoff position

Two cutoff positions for second baseman

Two cutoff positions for first baseman

Catcher

CUTOFF PLAYS
On balls hit deep to the outfield, teams often use a combination of throws from outfielder to infielder to the bases. Outfielders throw to "cutoff men," who then relay the ball to the bases or to home plate.

KEY
- LF to home
- Left-center to home
- CF to home
- Right-center to home
- RF to 3B
- RF to home

OUTFIELD THROWS
Outfielders use a longer arm swing and more body motion than infielders. They often run forward a step or two before throwing.

Eyes focus on the ball until it is firmly in the glove

INFIELD THROWS
Infielders have less time to throw and must make quick throws with less arm action.

Eyes face target

Glove hand stays tucked to body

FIELDING GROUND BALLS
This key skill is most often used by infielders. They try to field the ball between their legs, with the glove held low to the ground and the throwing hand waiting to grab the ball from the glove.

Throwing hand

Infielders often use a sidearm throwing motion

Feet and legs spread for good balance

Glove held like a scoop to receive ball

Batting

HITTING A BASEBALL HAS often been called the single most difficult feat in sports. The batter, or hitter, has just over a tenth of a second to begin a swing with a round bat at a round ball moving at more than 90 miles per hour in a variety of directions in both horizontal and vertical planes. In another quarter of a second or so, the batter must bring the bat into a level position to meet the ball, all while adjusting to the speed and placement of the oncoming pitch. At this point, the bat itself may be moving in excess of 80 miles an hour. Finally, in about half a second, the swing is over and the ball is hit or missed. And then it begins all over again with the next batter or the next pitch. The very best practitioners of this skill are successful only about three times in 10 at-bats. Another way of looking at how hard hitting is: The best at it fail seven times out of 10.

GETTING A GRIP
Batters often wipe the handles of their bats with a sticky pine tar rag to create a firmer grip.

Firm grip, but not too tight, with hands relaxed

Eyes look for the release point, head remains still

Front shoulder points toward pitcher

Righthanded batters have their left hand at the bottom of the grip; lefties do it in reverse

Most players try to keep their front elbow up as the swing begins

IN AND OUT OF THE STRIKE ZONE
Baseball players, coaches, and broadcasters use a wide variety of sometimes colorful phrases – examples of which are shown below – to describe the location of various pitches. Blue dots represent pitches in the strike zone; red dots are called balls.

KEY
● strikes ● balls ▪ strike zone

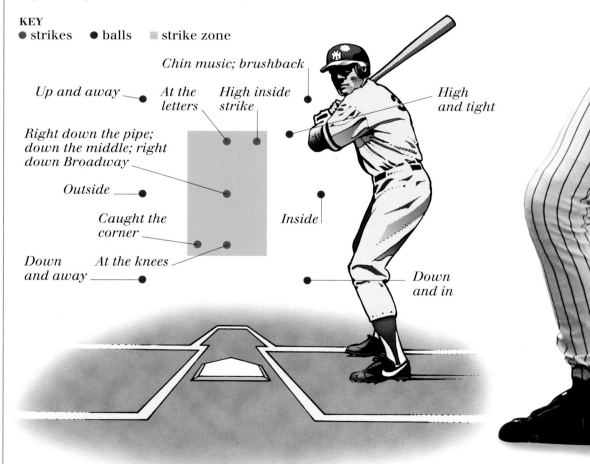

Chin music; brushback

Up and away

At the letters

High inside strike

High and tight

Right down the pipe; down the middle; right down Broadway

Outside

Caught the corner

Inside

Down and away

At the knees

Down and in

Front leg lifts or slides to begin stride

Weight on inside part of foot

AT THE PLATE
Dozens of movements from head to toe must be coordinated to create a good baseball swing. Endless hours of practice are the key to building the swing, although some players possess an innate talent for hitting a pitch.

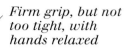

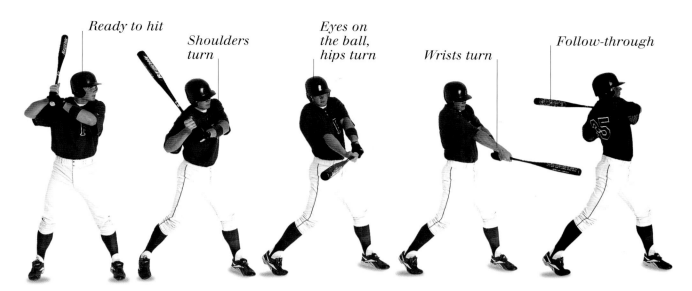

Ready to hit

Shoulders turn

Eyes on the ball, hips turn

Wrists turn

Follow-through

LEVEL SWING

The classic baseball swing has several key parts. It begins with a solid stance, with feet about shoulder-width apart. As the bat is swung, the shoulders turn, the hips turn, the hands follow the hips, and at or just after contact the wrists snap over to provide power. The eyes try to follow the ball throughout the swing, while a full follow-through keeps hitters balanced.

The release point does not vary much from pitch to pitch

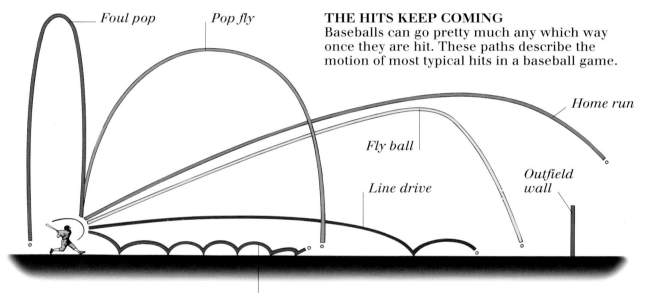

Foul pop

Pop fly

THE HITS KEEP COMING

Baseballs can go pretty much any which way once they are hit. These paths describe the motion of most typical hits in a baseball game.

Home run

Fly ball

Line drive

Outfield wall

Ground ball, grounder, bouncer

RELEASE POINT

Batters watch carefully for the point in space from which the pitcher releases the ball.

TAKING STOCK OF STANCES

There are as many batting stances as there are batters. Players experiment constantly to find the stance, swing, grip, bat, and more that works best for them...anything to get a hit. These three players were successful with unorthodox stances.

Mel Ott hit 511 career home runs using an exaggerated leg lift before each swing

NL all-time hit leader Stan Musial "peeked" over his shoulder and kept his hands close to his body

Seven-time batting champ Rod Carew held his bat much flatter than most hitters

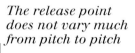

Pad protects ankle and top of foot from foul tips

EXTRA PADDING

Batters may wear a variety of extra pads on their arms and legs.

FOUR-SEAM FASTBALL

TWO-SEAM FASTBALL

CURVEBALL

Pitching

PITCHERS STAND 60 FEET, SIX INCHES away from home plate on a mound of dirt raised about 10 inches above the level of the infield. Each play in baseball starts with the pitcher throwing, or pitching the baseball toward home plate. The pitcher's job? Get the batter out in any way possible. To accomplish this mission, pitchers use a variety of tools. The speed of their pitches is their greatest weapon; top pitchers can throw the ball nearly 100 miles per hour. Often, however, they vary the speeds of their pitches to keep hitters guessing. Using different grips on the ball and movements with their hands and wrists, pitchers make the ball curve, dip, slide, knuckle (wobble unpredictably), or hop. They change the angle of their release or their leg motion to confuse the batter. Until 1934, it was even legal for the pitcher to put a foreign substance (such as saliva, petroleum jelly, or dirt) on the ball to make it move in unpredictable ways. Hall of Fame pitcher Warren Spahn once said, "Hitting is the art of timing. Pitching is the art of upsetting timing."

HOW PITCHES MOVE OVER HOME PLATE

KEY
- ■ curveball
- ■ two-seam fastball or sinker
- ■ changeup
- ■ four-seam fastball
- ■ cutter or slider

CIRCLE CHANGE-UP

KNUCKLEBALL

GETTING A GRIP
Pitchers use the position of their hand on the baseball to help determine how a pitch moves. Pressure is put on the raised seams to make the ball spin certain ways.

The wind-up begins

Eyes lock in on target

Arm reaches back; palm faces down

Front foot reaches toward home plate

Arm moves into throwing position

Leg closest to home plate raises up

Back foot drives off rubber

Long stride toward home

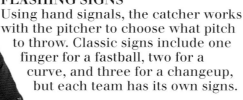

Hand held between legs

FLASHING SIGNS
Using hand signals, the catcher works with the pitcher to choose what pitch to throw. Classic signs include one finger for a fastball, two for a curve, and three for a changeup, but each team has its own signs.

Glove shields view of fingers from baserunners

NO SWEAT
A bag of powdery rosin is kept on the back of the mound; pitchers use it to keep their hands dry.

TYPICAL PITCH MOTION, SIDE VIEW

KEY
curveball
fastball
sinker or slider

Unusual release point can make this motion more difficult to hit

Hand follows elbow toward target

HERE'S THE PITCH...
This sequence shows a typical pitching motion, or delivery. Every pitcher has his own unique delivery, but there are certain fundamentals. These include eyes on the target, driving the back foot off the rubber, and leading with the elbow.

THROWING SIDEARM
This is another way to pitch. With a whip-like motion, the hand and arm throw the ball from below shoulder level instead of from above.

Elbow at 90 degrees to ground

Back foot comes off rubber as ball is released from hand

Hand at ear level

Eyes on target

Chest turns to become square to target, stays over knee

Weight moving toward front leg

Foot leaves rubber as ball leaves hand

Planted foot supports weight and provides balance

Baserunning

THE MOMENT A BATTER HITS THE ball fair, he becomes a baserunner and must try to advance as many bases as he can. After reaching base safely, baserunners can advance to the next bases in a myriad of ways. The most obvious way is on a teammate's hit or walk. The next most common method is the stolen base, in which a player simply runs to the next base before the defense can tag him out. A speedy basestealer can play havoc with a pitcher and with a defense. While speed is one key to being a baserunner, baseball smarts are equally important. Knowing when to advance from first to third on a single, when to try to score on a sacrifice fly, and when to get in a rundown to let your teammate advance can mean the difference between a high-scoring rally and an inning-killing out.

BASES
Official plastic- or canvas-covered bases, also referred to as "bags," are 15 inches square and three to five inches thick.

HOW THEY STICK
At the professional and collegiate level, bases are anchored to the field with square metal pegs.

Square pegs keep the bases from spinning when they are stepped on

Path of batted ball

Batter as baserunner

Path of runner

Batting

RUNNING THE BASES
Baserunners rarely run in a straight line. The purple line above describes an ideal, circular route taken by a player who has hit a long triple. "Rounding" the bases lets a runner stay at top speed even while turning the corners of the bases; it's easier to run in a circle than a square.

HE'S IN THERE!
This baserunner executes a picture-perfect "figure 4" slide. The front leg reaches out for the base, while the back leg folds under, forming a numeral 4. Ideally, the runner slides on his leg, hip, and buttock, with the arm used for balance rather than support.

Fielders can block a baserunner with their bodies if they have the ball

Fielders also have to know when to get out of the way to avoid a collision

Runner's front foot extends to touch base

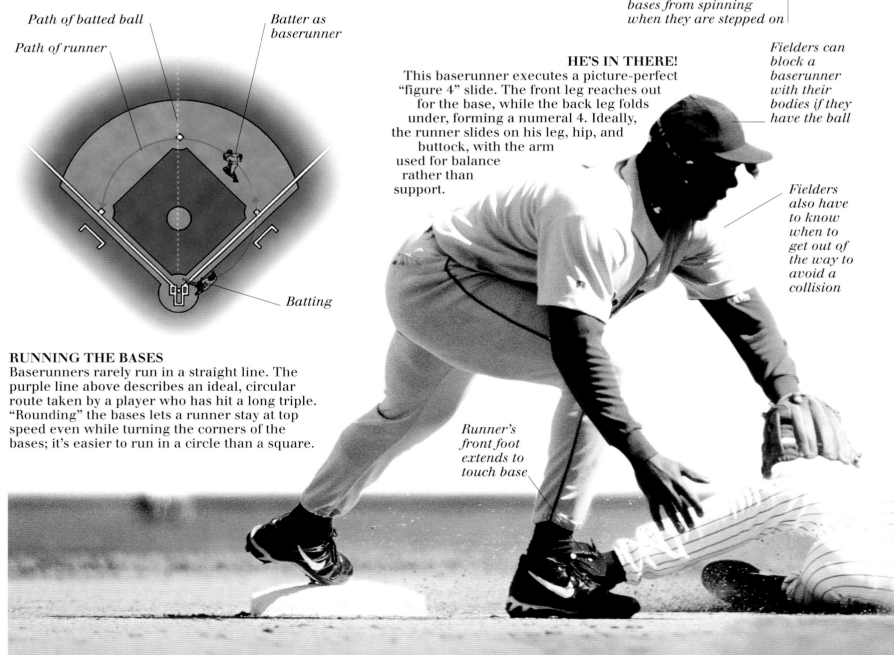

In headfirst slide, hands touch base first

ANOTHER WAY TO SLIDE
All-time stolen base leader Rickey Henderson demonstrates the headfirst slide. Some players prefer to dive for the base with their hands, sliding on their chest. Some people believe a headfirst slide increases the risk of injury to the baserunner.

Runners use the base as a starting block to begin running

JUST THE CORNER
Baserunners are taught to hit the corner as they run. This helps avoid slipping on the base and shortens the path around the bases,

Base anchored to field

Batting helmets must be worn while on the bases

Left, or back arm, out for support

HOW A BASE IS STOLEN
A baserunner can steal a base at any time. This is nearly always done as the pitcher throws toward home plate. The catcher must then catch the ball and quickly throw it to a fielder covering the base. Below is a typical sequence.

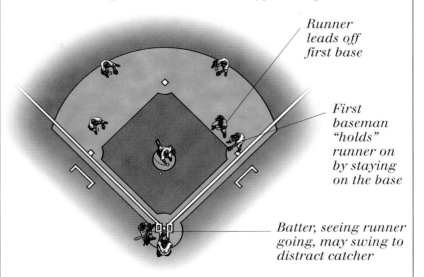

Runner leads off first base

First baseman "holds" runner on by staying on the base

Batter, seeing runner going, may swing to distract catcher

1. PITCH THROWN TOWARD HOME PLATE

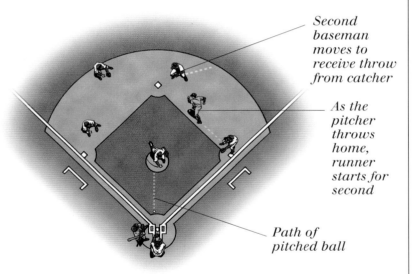

Second baseman moves to receive throw from catcher

As the pitcher throws home, runner starts for second

Path of pitched ball

2. RUNNER TAKES OFF FOR SECOND BASE

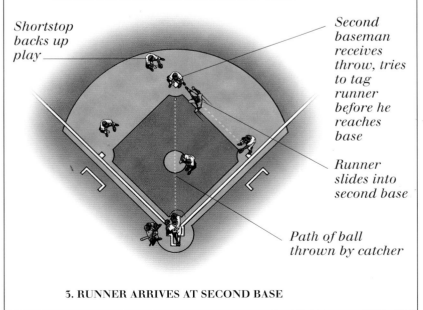

Shortstop backs up play

Second baseman receives throw, tries to tag runner before he reaches base

Runner slides into second base

Path of ball thrown by catcher

3. RUNNER ARRIVES AT SECOND BASE

Managers and coaches

THE MANAGER MAKES ALL the on-field decisions, including who will play what position, what order the players will bat in, and when a pitcher should come out of a game. Managers are in a constant strategic battle with their opposite number, trying to outguess and outmaneuver the other team by moving players, changing lineups, and using a wide variety of special plays. Managers are assisted by several coaches. Most teams have special coaches for pitching, hitting, and working with the bullpen, along with coaches who work at first and third base when a team is at bat. The manager consults with his coaches during a game, but the final call is always up to him. Modern baseball managers are under enormous pressure to succeed. A famous baseball saying sums up the manager's life: "There are two kinds of managers – winning managers and ex-managers."

GROUND RULES

Before each game, opposing managers or coaches meet with the umpires and one another to exchange lineup cards and go over the ground rules, which are rules unique to each ballpark.

TEAM ROSTER

Major League teams may keep 25 players on their active roster. The roster may change due to injuries, trades, minor league call-ups, or other player moves. Most teams keep 10 to 12 pitchers, a starter at each field position, a backup outfielder or two, a backup infielder or two, and a utility player who is adept at several positions. Careful handling of his players throughout a game and a season is the key responsibility of the team manager, working with his coaches and the team's front office.

Uniform number · *Player's name* · *Position*

What a player bats and throws: righthanded (R) or lefthanded (L); some players are switch hitters (S)

Height

Weight

Date of birth

Players are listed at their primary position, but may play more than one

2000 Team Roster

PITCHERS

NO.	PLAYER	POS	B-T	HT	WT	DOB
54	Mark Clark	P	R-R	6-5	235	5/12/68
30	Francisco Cordero	P	R-R	6-2	200	8/11/77
23	Tim Crabtree	P	R-R	6-4	220	10/13/69
32	Rick Helling	P	R-R	6-3	210	12/15/70
28	Esteban Loaiza	P	R-R	6-3	210	12/31/71
51	Mike Munoz	P	L-L	6-2	198	7/12/65
14	Darren Oliver	P	R-L	6-2	210	10/6/70
40	Matt Perisho	P	L-L	6-0	205	7/8/75
37	Kenny Rogers	P	L-L	6-1	217	11/10/64
43	Mike Venafro	P	L-L	5-10	180	8/2/73
35	John Wetteland	P	R-R	6-2	215	8/21/66
59	Jeff Zimmerman	P	R-R	6-1	200	8/9/72

BATTERS

NO.	PLAYER	POS	B-T	HT	WT	DOB
10	Luis Alicea	2B	S-R	5-9	176	7/29/65
27	Frank Catalanotto	2B	L-R	6-0	195	4/27/74
11	Royce Clayton	SS	R-R	6-0	183	1/2/70
3	Chad Curtis	OF	R-R	5-10	185	11/6/68
6	Tom Evans	3B	R-R	6-1	180	7/9/74
29	Rusty Greer	OF	L-L	6-0	195	1/21/69
33	Bill Haselman	C	R-R	6-3	223	5/25/66
18	Gabe Kapler	OF	R-R	6-2	208	8/31/75
21	Ruben Mateo	OF	R-R	6-0	185	2/10/78
25	Rafael Palmeiro	1B	L-L	6-0	190	9/24/64
7	Ivan Rodriguez	C	R-R	5-9	205	11/30/71
24	David Segui	1B	S-L	6/1	202	7/19/66
	Scott Sheldon	1B	R-R	6-3	215	11/20/68

FLASHING THE SIGNS

Baseball teams use a wide variety of signs – physical movements by coaches – to send instructions and strategy to players on the field. Signs are often used by the third base coach to relay instructions to the batter.

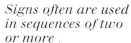

Signs are changed constantly to avoid being stolen by opponents

Signs include touching or wiping parts of the body

Signs often are used in sequences of two or more

MAKING THE LINEUP

A manager's most important job is to set his team's batting order, or lineup, before each game. He gives this official lineup card to the umpire before the game. It lists the players in batting order, along with bench players, including pitchers. A manager must also be cognizant of the opposing team's lineup: Who does the other team have left on the bench? Who is coming up two, three, or four batters from now? How does his team match up with the opponent?

Leadoff hitter: disciplined, expected to get on base often

No. 2 hitter: handles the bat well, good at hit-and-run

No. 3 hitter: best hitter on the team, has power and speed

Cleanup hitter: batting fourth, normally a team's best power hitter

Pitchers are listed last; pitchers don't bat in the AL

Players on the bench are listed by how they bat, either left- or righthanded

The names of switch hitters are shown this way

Pitchers are listed by which arm they throw with

Lefthanded pitchers are less common than righties; often a team keeps only one or two in the lineup

As players enter the game, managers draw a line through their name

These numbers indicate what position a player plays on the field

Designated hitter, used only in the AL

No. 5 batter is the second best power hitter

No. 6 batter often acts as a second leadoff man

No. 7 batter handles bat well, can keep an inning alive

Nos. 8 and 9 batters are the weakest hitters on the team; in the NL, pitchers nearly always bat last

Keeping track of which pitchers remain available to both teams is part of the pitching coach's job

LINE-UP CARD   DATE: 9/20

ORIOLES
1 — Alomar — 4
2 — Anderson — 8
3 — W. Greene — 9
4 — Palmeiro — 3
5 — Pickering — DH
6 — Minor — 5
7 — Surhoff — 7
8 — Webster — 2
9 — Bordick — 6
P — Johns — 1

VISITING CLUB
1 — Knoblauch — 4
2 — Jeter — 6
3 — Williams — 8
4 — Davis — DH
5 — Posada — 2
6 — 2 Raines — 7
7 — Curtis — 9
8 — Lowell — 8
9 — Sojo — 3
P — Hernandez — 1

LH   EXTRA   RH
Becker   Voiles C. Greene
          Reboulet Forbes
Baines   Hairston
          Mouton Davis
          Clyburn Davis
          Kingsale Ripken

LH   EXTRA   RH
          Martinez   Bush
          Leaue   Spencer
          O'Neill   Brosius.
          Strawberry Girardi
                      Figga

LH EXTRA PITCHERS RH
Key   Drabek Smith
Rhodes   Coppinger
Orosco   Russell
         Mills
         Benitez

LH EXTRA PITCHERS RH
          Grusile Buddi
Lloyd   Bradley Tessm
Stanton   Borowski
          Holmes Nelso
          Mendoza

31

Umpires

UMPIRES ARE CHARGED WITH enforcing the rules of baseball. They impartially decide if a player is out or safe, if a pitch is a strike or a ball, and if a batted ball is foul or fair. In baseball's early days, the umpire worked from behind the pitcher or to the side of home plate, and he usually worked alone. The traditional umpires' hand signals were developed in the 1890s when a deaf player, William Hoy, played professionally and couldn't hear the umps' calls. Today, four umpires work Major League games, with six umpires used at All-Star and postseason games, and from one to three umpires at lower levels of baseball. Umpires have a difficult job; they must make dozens of split-second decisions under the unforgiving eyes of both teams, the fans in the stands, and, often, the slow-motion instant replay of television. Universally known as "the men in blue" for their traditional uniforms, umpires have but one charge: In the immortal words of Hall of Fame umpire Bill Klem, to "call 'em as I see 'em."

Metal and leather face mask

Throat protector

Chest protector worn under shirt

Bags on belt contain brush, extra balls

Shin guards worn under pants

Steel-toed shoes protect feet from foul tips

HOME PLATE UMPIRE
Wearing many pieces of protective gear, home plate umpires call balls and strikes, make calls on plays at home plate, and rule on fair or foul balls between home plate and first and third bases.

OLD-STYLE PROTECTION
When umpires moved behind the plate, they wore protective pads similar to catchers'.

Short brim of cap fits under face mask

Umpire's uniforms once included neckties

Inflatable pad, circa 1940s

THE BRUSH-OFF
Umpires carry small brushes to clean home plate. By tradition, and for politeness, they always face the fans, rather than the players, when dusting off the plate.

STRIKE BALL

OUT

INNING

Home plate umpire keeps the count, but other umpires keep track, too

Thumb wheel

KEEPING COUNT
Umpires use handheld devices like this one to help them keep count of balls, strikes, outs, and innings. Modern scoreboards have made these devices more backup than primary.

UMPIRES' POSITIONS

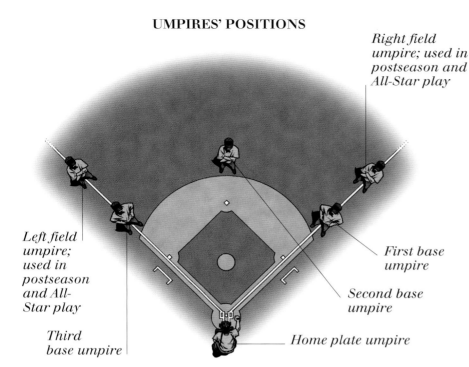

Right field umpire; used in postseason and All-Star play

Left field umpire; used in postseason and All-Star play

Third base umpire

First base umpire

Second base umpire

Home plate umpire

HOME PLATE UMPIRE'S SIGNALS

The umpire's traditional blue shirt

STRIKE!
Plate umpires signal strikes with an upraised hand or fist or by pointing to one side. No signal is given for a called ball.

STRIKE THREE!
On a called third strike, an umpire can show a little flair, perhaps by emphatically "punching out" the batter.

Major League umpires have uniform numbers like players

IN POSITION
Home plate umpires crouch behind the catcher before each pitch. They try to stay low to get a good view of the pitch as it crosses home plate.

YOU'RE OUTTA HERE
Umpires have the power to eject players, coaches, and managers for protesting calls too vehemently or for unsportsmanlike conduct. Most umpires point at the offending party and then point off the field. Some umpires are more dramatic when ejecting players.

Umpires traditionally wear long gray pants

FOUL/TIME OUT
Umpires on the base lines signal a foul ball by holding their hands above their heads. This signal also calls time out.

FAIR BALL
This third base umpire points to fair territory to indicate a ball was batted fair. Base umpires straddle the baseline to get a good view of the hit.

Colored undershirt

Black athletic shoes

HE'S OUT!
To signal an out, whether by force or tag, umpires normally hold up a closed fist. Some may point at the runner while "punching them out."

HE'S SAFE!
When a player reaches a base safely, the umpire holds his arms out this way. He may repeat this several times for emphasis on close plays.

Ballparks

BABEBALL IS PLAYED IN ballparks, sometimes called stadiums. Ballpark design has evolved in waves over the past century. Baseball's early homes were little more than fields surrounded by a fence. Ballparks in big cities were built to conform to crowded city streets, which often created unusual shapes. They began to get larger when Yankee Stadium was built in 1923. By the 1960s, a circular, multipurpose, yet antiseptic style dominated. In the past 10 years, more than a dozen new ballparks have opened up as Major League teams try to increase fan enjoyment – and revenue. Ironically, most recently built parks seek to harken back to the early city stadiums, with quirks like small hills in the outfield, huge outfield walls, and lots of brick. However, today's new stadiums also boast luxury suites and all the modern conveniences.

Small grandstand

Diamond is set up in corner of larger park

EARLY BASEBALL SITE
More than a simple field, but not quite a stadium, this ballpark from the 1880s shows how spectators crowded close to the field, sometimes standing near the foul lines.

The Green Monster is a 37-foot wall in left field

FENWAY PARK
Opened in 1912, Fenway Park in Boston is the oldest ballpark in the Major Leagues. The home of the Red Sox is revered for its history, charm, and quirks. While the team hopes to move into a bigger stadium, traditionalists are fighting to save the park.

Upper deck seating

Light tower

Scoreboards above outfield seats

WRIGLEY FIELD
Chicago's Wrigley Field has an unusual ballpark feature: ivy covering its brick outfield walls.

CLASSIC OLD DESIGN

This overhead view of Ebbets Field in Brooklyn (which no longer stands), home of the Dodgers from 1913 to 1957, shows how the first stadiums were built to fit into city neighborhoods, with the building's boundaries defined by the streets.

CLASSIC MODERN DESIGN

Turner Field in Atlanta opened for the hometown Braves in 1997 amid a spate of new stadium construction. Originally built for the 1996 Summer Olympics, it is a classic multi-tiered baseball stadium, with stands rising from the playing field in levels. Outfield bleachers complete the modern classic design. Seats are angled so that all face the center of the field.

Outfield bleacher seats

INDOOR-OUTDOOR STADIUM

Toronto's Skydome, home of the Blue Jays, was the first baseball stadium with a completely retractable roof. On days with bad weather, the enormous roof slides on rails to cover the field and the fans.

Dirt around bases allows for safe sliding

ARTIFICIAL TURF

Some modern stadiums, and all indoor stadiums, use artificial turf instead of grass, which won't grow indoors. Most varities of the product are plastic, often sewn into mats to resemble real grass or turf. Players don't enjoy playing on artificial turf; the ball bounces higher and faster and the ground is harder.

SIDE SCHEMATIC OF TYPICAL NEW STADIUM

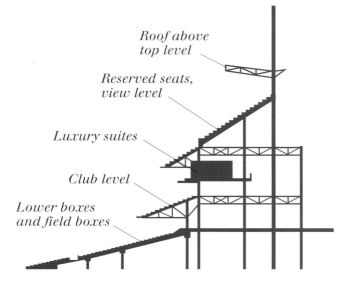

Roof above top level

Reserved seats, view level

Luxury suites

Club level

Lower boxes and field boxes

SAN FRANCISCO'S NEW PACIFIC BELL PARK

Keeping score

THE MOST IMPORTANT PART of keeping score in a baseball game is noting the number of runs each team has scored. But there is much more to it than that. Using a unique set of symbols and codes, fans, players, coaches, and broadcasters record each at-bat so that the events of a complete game can be reduced to a single sheet of paper. Before the advent of television or radio, an early version of this system was used to transmit information via telegraph to huge scoreboards in places such as New York's Times Square. Crowds would gather to "watch" the game unfold in symbols, signs, and numbers. There is also an official scorer, whose responsibility it is to interpret and record the action taking place. The official scorer also makes judgment calls, including whether a play is a hit or an error, what is a wild pitch, and what's an earned run. In this capacity, the scorer can have a significant impact on a player's statistics and on which baseball records stand or fall.

HENRY CHADWICK
Chadwick, a writer and reporter in the late 1800s, is credited with popularizing most baseball statistics and inventing scorekeeping.

OFFICIAL SCORER
The official scorer sits in the press box along with radio, TV, and print reporters. The league president designates a local reporter to score each game.

VIDEO STARS
Most stadiums now have scoreboards with high-tech video screens.

THE SCOREBOARD
Fans in stadiums keep track of game events, as well as scores of other games, by watching the scoreboard. This scoreboard in Chicago's Wrigley Field is one of baseball's classics.

Clock showing time of day

Loudspeakers

Other National League scores

Line scores of other games; home teams are listed second

Game that will start later in the day; no score recorded yet

Uniform number of starting pitcher

Uniform number of relief pitcher

Line score of Cubs' game being played at Wrigley Field

4-3: indicates ground ball caught by second baseman, thrown to first baseman for the out

Pinch-hitter; "3" means inning he was inserted

Filled-in space indicates run scored, in this case on a home run (HR)

Player's uniform number, last name

Number in circle indicates out number in the inning

American League scores

KEEPING SCORE

This sample shows one method of keeping score during a game. Individual batters' results are recorded using the symbols below, and each defensive position is given a number. Knowledgeable fans can see at a glance what has happened in this game.

NO.	GIANTS	POS.	1	2	3	4	5
7	Benard	8	4-3		CS2-6		
23	Burks - 3						
32	Mueller	5	9		9		
25	Bonds	7	HR		3G		
21	Kent	4	K		9		
6	Snow	3		6-4	PB 9		
1	Rios	9	WP		7		
35	Aurilia	6	9		K		
29	Estalella	2	SB BB				
48	Ortiz	1	4L				

Caught stealing, catcher (2) throws to shortstop (6)

Right fielder's position number shows fly-ball out

Backward K means struck out without swinging at third strike

Lines are used to indicate player's path around base; this player reached base via a walk (BB) and then stole (SB) second base

Slash indicates last batter of inning

SCORING SYMBOLS

◇	Single
◇	Double
◇	Triple
HR	Home run
E	Error
BB	Base on balls
K	Strikeout
FC	Fielder's choice
SB	Stolen base
SF	Sacrifice fly
CS	Caught stealing
WP	Wild pitch
PB	Passed ball
BK	Balk

POSITION NUMBERS

P	1	SS	6
C	2	LF	7
1B	3	CF	8
2B	4	RF	9
3B	5		

AMERICAN

	SAN DIEGO		N			G						
	SEATTLE		I			A						
	COLORADO		T			M						
	ANAHEIM		E			E						
	SAN FRANCISCO											
	OAKLAND											
1	8	KANSAS CITY	1	0	0	0	0	3	0	1	2	
7	8	CINCINNATI	0	1	2	0	0	0	0	0		
4		BALTIMORE										
12		FLORIDA										
6		CHICAGO	0	0	0	0	3	0				
9		ST. LOUIS	0	0	1	1	0	0				
SP	RP	INNING	1	2	3	4	5	6	7	8	9	10

Indicates games will be played later that night

Official scorecard from 1888 Cincinnati Red Stockings

Star pitcher Leon Viau

Note spelling of "base ball" as two words

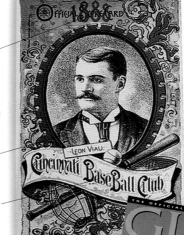

GET YOUR SCORECARDS!

From the game's earliest days, fans have bought scorecards at the ballpark on which they record the action of the game, look up player information, or read about the team or the stadium.

San Francisco's PacBell Park, opened in 2000

Current batter, and results of his previous at-bats

Statistics

CYBERSTATS
Millions of fans now get their baseball scores, stats, and information at Web sites, such as majorleaguebaseball.com.

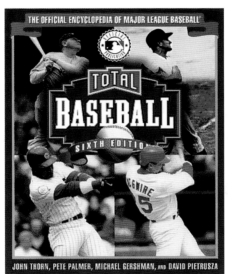

THE OFFICIAL RECORD
The official record book of Major League Baseball is published as *Total Baseball*. At 6.5 pounds and more than 2,500 pages, it is an all-encompassing compendium of baseball statistics and historical information.

A MASSIVE ARRAY OF STATISTICS RECORDS the accomplishments and events of every baseball player, team, game, series, season, career, and more. From baseball's earliest days, the game's players have been judged as much on their "numbers" as on their skill. In fact, the numbers are used as proof of skill and talent. A .300 hitter is a high-quality professional batter. A pitcher with an ERA (earned run average) below 3.00 is regarded as a staff ace. On the other end of the spectrum, a player who is "below the Mendoza line" has a paltry batting average below .200 (named for Mario Mendoza, who played in the 1970s and early '80s). Along with being a source of constant discussion (and memorization) by fans, statistics are strategic tools used by managers and coaches to prepare for their opponents. Stats help a manager know, for instance, which pitcher will fare better against lefthanded batters in night games in May. The possibilities are as endless as the numbers.

BY THE NUMBERS
A line of type in the newspaper or a magazine quickly sums up a pitcher's (top) or a player's (bottom) season, using a variety of statistical categories.

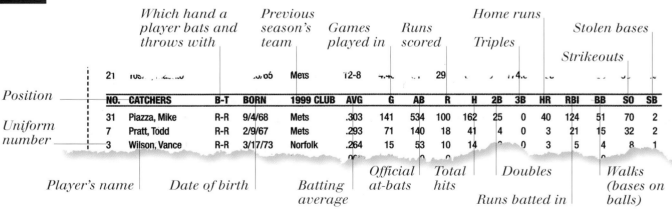

Uniform number — *Pitcher's name* — *Win-loss record* — *Earned-run average* — *Games started* — *Saves* — *Innings pitched* — *Walks (also known as bases on balls, or BB)* — *Earned runs allowed*

NO.	PITCHERS	B-T	BORN	1999 CLUB	W-L	ERA	G	GS	CG	SV	IP	H	R	ER	BB	SO
19	Appier, Kevin	R-R	12/6/67	Oakland	7-5	5.77	12	12	0	0	68.2	77	50	44	33	53
				Kansas City	9-9	4.87	22	22	1	0	140.1	153	81	76	51	78
40	DuBose, Eric	L-L	5/15/76	Midland	4-2	5.49	21	14	0		77.0	89	57	47	44	68
49	Enochs, Chris	R-R	10/11/75	Midland	3-5	10.00	13							50	34	33
62	Gregg, Kevin	R-R	?78	Midland	4-7	3.74										
32	Ham...															

Games pitched in — *Complete games* — *Hits allowed* — *Strikeouts* — *Runs allowed*

Which hand a player bats and throws with — *Previous season's team* — *Games played in* — *Runs scored* — *Triples* — *Home runs* — *Stolen bases* — *Strikeouts*

NO.		B-T	BORN	1999 CLUB		G			R						SO	SB
21	Tos...			Mets	12-8		29				11.4					

Position — *Uniform number* — *Player's name* — *Date of birth* — *Batting average*

NO.	CATCHERS	B-T	BORN	1999 CLUB	AVG	G	AB	R	H	2B	3B	HR	RBI	BB	SO	SB
31	Piazza, Mike	R-R	9/4/68	Mets	.303	141	534	100	162	25	0	40	124	51	70	2
7	Pratt, Todd	R-R	2/9/67	Mets	.293	71	140	18	41	4	0	3	21	15	32	2
3	Wilson, Vance	R-R	3/17/73	Norfolk	.264	15	53	10	14		0	3	5	4	8	1

Official at-bats — *Total hits* — *Doubles* — *Walks (bases on balls)* — *Runs batted in*

HOW TO CALCULATE IMPORTANT BASEBALL STATISTICS

BATTING AVERAGE
Hits÷At-Bats. Example:
$$\frac{125 \text{ H}}{435 \text{ AB}} = .287$$

EARNED RUN AVERAGE
(Earned runs x 9)÷Innings Pitched. Example:
$$\frac{(62 \text{ ER x } 9)}{251 \text{ IP}} = 2.22$$

SLUGGING AVERAGE
Total Bases÷At-Bats. Example:
$$\frac{349 \text{ TB}}{598 \text{ AB}} = .583$$

ON-BASE PERCENTAGE
(Hits + Walks + Hit by Pitch)÷ (AB + Walks + HBP + Sacrifices + Sacrifice Flys)
Example:
$$\frac{(172 \text{ H} + 47 \text{ BB} + 6 \text{ HBP})}{(586 \text{ AB} + 47 \text{ BB} + 6 \text{ HBP} + 9 \text{ S} + 6 \text{ SF})} = .344$$

DAILY STANDINGS

Who's in first? The daily standings track the position of each team in its division during the regular season. The team with the most wins in each division makes the playoffs, as does one wild-card team – the team with the best record that did not win its division.

FINAL 1999 MAJOR LEAGUE STANDINGS

AMERICAN LEAGUE

EAST	Won	Lost	Pct.	GB
New York	98	64	.605	—
Boston	94	68	.580	4
Toronto	84	78	.519	14
Baltimore	78	84	.481	20
Tampa Bay	69	93	.426	29

CENTRAL	Won	Lost	Pct.	GB
Cleveland	97	65	.599	—
Chicago	75	86	.466	21.5
Detroit	69	92	.429	27.5
Kansas City	64	97	.398	32.5
Minnesota	63	97	.394	33

WEST	Won	Lost	Pct.	GB
Texas	95	67	.586	—
Oakland	87	75	.537	8
Seattle	79	83	.488	16
Anaheim	70	92	.432	25

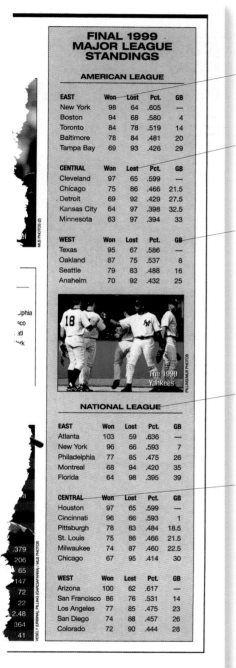

The 1999 Yankees

NATIONAL LEAGUE

EAST	Won	Lost	Pct.	GB
Atlanta	103	59	.636	—
New York	96	66	.593	7
Philadelphia	77	85	.475	26
Montreal	68	94	.420	35
Florida	64	98	.395	39

CENTRAL	Won	Lost	Pct.	GB
Houston	97	65	.599	—
Cincinnati	96	66	.593	1
Pittsburgh	78	83	.484	18.5
St. Louis	75	86	.466	21.5
Milwaukee	74	87	.460	22.5
Chicago	67	95	.414	30

WEST	Won	Lost	Pct.	GB
Arizona	100	62	.617	—
San Francisco	86	76	.531	14
Los Angeles	77	85	.475	23
San Diego	74	88	.457	26
Colorado	72	90	.444	28

Wins

Losses

Games behind the division leader; calculated by halving the total of the differences between wins and losses

Standings are shown by league

Three divisions in each league (through 2000)

BOX SCORE

The first place every baseball fan turns to in the morning paper is the box score from the previous night's game. Each game is summed up in a neat vertical box containing words, symbols, and numbers. This box score shows the San Diego Padres' 10-3 victory over the St. Louis Cardinals, in which St. Louis's Mark McGwire hit two home runs, the first of which was the 500th of his career. The invention of the box score is credited to Henry Chadwick, one of the most important early baseball writers.

Padres 10, Cardinals 3

Final score

Visiting team on top

Players listed in batting order, with position

Totals of each column of stats

Home team on bottom

The key stats: at-bats, runs, hits, runs batted in, walks, strikeouts, batting average

McGwire's line shows two hits in four at-bats, with two runs scored and two RBI

San Diego	AB	R	H	BI	BB	SO	Avg.
Veras 2b	4	2	0	0	1	1	.274
Gwynn rf	4	1	1	2	1	0	.316
RSanders lf	4	1	1	0	1	0	.298
Nevin 3b	5	1	2	0	0	0	.250
Joyner 1b	4	1	1	2	1	1	.250
Owens cf	4	2	2	0	1	0	.297
Hoffman p	1	0	0	0	0	0	.500
BDavis c	4	0	1	2	0	0	.304
Gomez ss	3	1	2	0	1	0	.240
Ashby p	2	0	0	1	1	0	.125
RRivera cf	1	1	1	0	0	0	.220
Totals	36	10	10	9	5	2	

St. Louis	AB	R	H	BI	BB	SO	Avg.
Drew cf	4	0	0	0	0	1	.261
McGee rf	4	0	0	0	0	1	.254
McGwire 1b	4	2	2	2	0	0	.279
Lankford lf	4	1	3	0	0	0	.307
Tatis 3b	3	0	1	0	1	1	.293
Renteria ss	4	0	0	1	0	1	.277
Paquette 2b	3	0	0	0	0	1	.333
Marrero c	1	0	0	0	0	0	.199
Luebbers p	1	0	0	0	0	0	.000
a-DHoward	1	0	0	0	0	0	.217
Acevedo p	0	0	0	0	0	0	.053
b-Polanco	1	0	0	0	0	0	.267
Mohler p	0	0	0	0	0	0	.000
Aybar p	0	0	0	0	0	0	.091
Totals	32	3	6	3	3	4	

San Diego	110 021 005	— 10	10 0
St. Louis	011 000 010	— 3	6 3

Line score shows runs by inning

Area for recording pinch-hitters

Various events in game are in bold

a-walked for Luebbers in the 5th. b-grounded out for Acevedo in the 7th.
E—Renteria (19), Paquette (2), Marrero (5). **LOB**—San Diego 6, St. Louis 5. **2B**—Gwynn (14), Nevin (12), Hoffman (1), Lankford (21). **HR**—McGwire 2 (44) off Ashby 2. **RBIs**—Gwynn 2 (43), Joyner (31), Hoffman 2 (2), Gomez 2 (6), McGwire 2 (101), Renteria (44). **SB**—Veras (20), RSanders 2 (26), Owens 2 (26), Drew (9). **S**—Ashby. **SF**—Gomez. **GIDP**—Renteria.
Runners left in scoring position—San Diego 4 (RSanders 2, Joyner, BDavis); St. Louis 2 (McGee, Luebbers). **Runners moved up**—Nevin, BDavis, Paquette.
DP—San Diego 1 (Gomez, Veras and Joyner).

For each event, the player who did it and new season total is listed; this shows Gwynn with two RBI, for a season total of 33

San Diego	IP	H	R	ER	BB	SO	NP	ERA
Ashby W, 10-5	7⅔	5	3	3	3	3	108	3.40
Hoffman S, 27	1⅓	1	0	0	0	1	19	2.89

St. Louis	IP	H	R	ER	BB	SO	NP	ERA
Luebbers L, 1-2	5	5	4	4	4	1	73	5.24
Acevedo	2	2	1	1	0	1	26	6.23
Mohler	1	0	0	0	0	0	15	4.89
Aybar	1	3	5	1	1	0	18	3.98

IBB—By Aybar (Joyner), by Ashby (Marrero). **U**—Nelson, Hirschbeck, Bell, Wegner. **T**—2:47. **Tickets sold**—45,106.

Pitcher's line scores: innings pitched, hits allowed, runs allowed, earned runs allowed, number of pitches, and season earned run average

Umpires' names

American League

THE AMERICAN LEAGUE WAS FOUNDED in 1901 by Ban Johnson, joining the established National League (the AL has been referred to ever since as the "junior circuit"). The AL grew out of the American Association, first founded 20 years earlier to offer beer sales and Sunday baseball, both of which the NL banned. The AL began with eight teams, five of which – the Boston Red Sox, Chicago White Sox, Cleveland Indians, Detroit Tigers, and Oakland (originally Philadelphia) Athletics – are still playing. In the early years, the AL was looked down upon by the older NL; in fact, the 1904 NL champion New York Giants refused to play the AL champion Boston Pilgrims in the World Series, which had been held for the first time only the year before. However, a string of AL World Series championships, led by the Red Sox and the New York Yankees, established the AL on a par with the NL. Today, the American League consists of 14 teams arranged (through the 2000 season, at least) in three divisions: East, Central, and West. The two leagues play under the same Major League Baseball rules with one significant difference: In the AL, teams use a designated hitter, known as the DH, to bat in place of the pitcher. Since the DH was instituted in 1973, purists have raged against this change to baseball tradition. The rule remains a sticking point in the drive to help unify the two leagues under one Major League Baseball management structure.

The team was called the California Angels until 1997

ANAHEIM ANGELS
Founded: 1961
Home: Edison Field, Anaheim, California
World Series titles: 0
Fast fact: Former team owner Gene Autry gained fame as a songwriter, movie actor, and singing cowboy.

The Orioles name comes from another pro team from the 1890s

BALTIMORE ORIOLES
Founded: 1954
Home: Oriole Park at Camden Yards, Baltimore, Maryland
World Series Titles: 3
Fast Fact: The Orioles franchise was the St. Louis Browns until 1954.

Among early names for the club: Pilgrims, Puritans, and Somersets

BOSTON RED SOX
Founded: 1901
Home: Fenway Park, Boston, Massachusetts
World Series Titles: 5
Fast Fact: Red Sox fans blame the "cursed" trade of Babe Ruth in 1919 for the fact that they haven't won a Series title since 1918.

Team was first known as White Stockings; changed to Sox in 1902

CHICAGO WHITE SOX
Founded: 1901
Home: New Comiskey Park, Chicago, Illinois
World Series titles: 2
Fast fact: In 1977, the club briefly experimented with short pants uniforms.

The Indians' mascot is known as Chief Wahoo

CLEVELAND INDIANS
Founded: 1901
Home: Jacobs Field, Cleveland, Ohio
World Series titles: 2
Fast fact: From 1903-14, the team was called Naps, for star Napoleon Lajoie.

Only original AL team still known by its first nickname

DETROIT TIGERS
Founded: 1901
Home: Comerica Park, Detroit, Michigan
World Series titles: 4
Fast fact: An 18-2 April helped the Tigers to their 1984 World Series crown.

KANSAS CITY ROYALS
Founded: 1969
Home: Kaufman Stadium, Kansas City, Missouri
World Series titles: 1
Fast fact: In 1996, the Royals switched from artificial to natural turf.

Named for Twin Cities, Minneapolis and St. Paul

MINNESOTA TWINS
Founded: 1961
Home: Minneapolis Metrodome, Minnesota
World Series titles: 3
Fast fact: Despite a plea from President Eisenhower, the Washington Senators moved to Minnesota in 1961.

Team was known as Highlanders from 1903-12

Oakland is the franchise's third home, after Philadelphia and Kansas City

Compass symbolizes the team's nautical nickname

NEW YORK YANKEES
Founded: 1903
Home: Yankee Stadium, Bronx, New York
World Series titles: 25
Fast fact: The Yankees' total of 25 World Series championships is more than twice as many as any other team.

OAKLAND ATHLETICS
Founded: 1901
Home: Network Associates Coliseum, Oakland, California
World Series titles: 9
Fast fact: The Athletics are noted for wearing unusual white baseball shoes.

SEATTLE MARINERS
Founded: 1977
Home: Safeco Field, Seattle, Washington
World Series titles: 0
Fast fact: The Mariners' first winning season didn't come until 1991.

A devil ray is an aquatic animal related to the manta ray

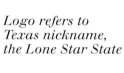

Logo refers to Texas nickname, the Lone Star State

Maple leaf is the national symbol of Canada

TAMPA BAY DEVIL RAYS
Founded: 1998
Home: Tropicana Field, St. Petersburg, Florida
World Series titles: 0
Fast fact: In 1999, Wade Boggs got his 3,000th career hit while with Tampa Bay.

TEXAS RANGERS
Founded: 1960
Home: The Ballpark at Arlington, Texas
World Series titles: 0
Fast fact: Club moved to Texas in 1972 from Washington, D.C.

TORONTO BLUE JAYS
Founded: 1977
Home: Skydome, Toronto, Ontario
World Series titles: 2
Fast fact: Their 1992 championship was the first by a Canadian team.

AMERICAN LEAGUE TEAMS ACROSS NORTH AMERICA

Seattle · Minneapolis · Toronto · Detroit · Boston · Chicago · Cleveland · New York · Kansas City · Baltimore · Oakland · Anaheim · Arlington · Tampa Bay

National League

THE OLDER OF BASEBALL'S TWO leagues was formed in 1876 out of the five-year-old National Association, the first professional league. The NL began with eight teams, with the westernmost franchise in St. Louis. Two clubs were expelled after one season and the number of league members fluctuated for most of the late 1800s. Three clubs – the Cincinnati Red Stockings (later Reds), the Chicago Cubs (originally the White Stockings), and the Boston (later Milwaukee and Atlanta) Braves – remain as original members of the NL. Today's NL does not use the designated hitter, as the American League does.

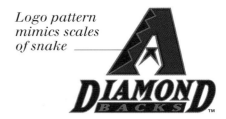

Logo pattern mimics scales of snake

ARIZONA DIAMONDBACKS
Founded: 1998
Home: Bank One Ballpark, Phoenix, Arizona
World Series titles: 0
Fast fact: The D-Backs' stadium has a swimming pool in the rightfield bleachers.

Team logo inspired fans' "tomahawk chop" cheer

ATLANTA BRAVES
Founded: 1871
Home: Turner Field, Atlanta, Georgia
World Series titles: 2
Fast Fact: The Braves are the only club to field a team in every season of professional baseball since 1871.

Current nickname was first used in 1899

CHICAGO CUBS
Founded: 1870
Home: Wrigley Field, Chicago, Illinois
World Series titles: 2
Fast fact: The Cubs have represented the same city longer than any other Major League team.

Original team, the Red Stockings, was the first pro team in 1869

CINCINNATI REDS
Founded: 1871
Home: Cinergy Field, Cincinnati, Ohio
World Series titles: 5
Fast fact: Reds' sleeveless jerseys were inspired by 1950s slugger Ted Kluszewski, whose massive arms made cuts necessary.

Rockies' home park is highest in the Majors

COLORADO ROCKIES
Founded: 1993
Home: Coors Field, Denver, Colorado
World Series titles: 0
Fast fact: The Rockies attracted an all-time Major League record 4.5 million fans during the team's inaugural season.

A marlin is a large ocean-going sportfish renowned for its power and speed

FLORIDA MARLINS
Founded: 1993
Home: Pro Player Stadium, Miami, Florida
World Series titles: 1
Fast fact: Their 1997 Series title was the fastest ever for an expansion team.

Houston's aerospace connections led to the team's name

HOUSTON ASTROS
Founded: 1962
Home: Enron Field, Houston, Texas
World Series titles: 0
Fast fact: Originally the Colt .45s, the Astros became first pro team to play indoors at the Houston Astrodome.

Name comes from Trolley-Dodgers, nickname for Brooklynites

LOS ANGELES DODGERS
Founded: 1883
Home: Dodger Stadium, Los Angeles, California
World Series titles: 6
Fast fact: A 1958 move from Brooklyn made them the first team west of St. Louis.

Why Brewers? Milwaukee is famous for beer

MILWAUKEE BREWERS
Founded: 1968
Home: Miller Park, Milwaukee, Wisconsin
World Series titles: 0
Fast fact: Club moved to its current home after one season as the Seattle Pilots.

Team name inspired by Expo '67 held in Montreal

MONTREAL EXPOS
Founded: 1969
Home: Olympic Stadium, Montreal, Quebec
World Series titles: 0
Fast fact: The Expos are the only team to broadcast games regularly in French.

Mets is short for Metropolitans

Cracked Liberty Bell is important city symbol

Team is colloquially known as the Bucs, short for Buccaneers

NEW YORK METS
Founded: 1962
Home: Shea Stadium, Queens, New York
World Series titles: 2
Fast fact: The Mets' 120 losses in 1962 were the most in a season in the 1900s.

PHILADELPHIA PHILLIES
Founded: 1883
Home: Veterans Stadium, Philadelphia, Pennsylvania
World Series titles: 1
Fast fact: The Phillies' 1980 Series title came 97 years after their founding.

PITTSBURGH PIRATES
Founded: 1883
Home: Three Rivers Stadium, Pittsburgh, Pennsylvania
World Series titles: 5
Fast fact: The Pirates lost to the Red Sox in the first World Series in 1903.

After seasons as the Browns and the Perfectos, team became the Cardinals in 1901

Nickname inspired by Franciscan priests who founded California missions

Team known as Gothams until the 1885 manager called them "my Giants"

ST. LOUIS CARDINALS
Founded: 1881
Home: Busch Stadium, St. Louis, Missouri
World Series titles: 9
Fast fact: The Cardinals trail only the Yankees in number of World Series titles.

SAN DIEGO PADRES
Founded: 1969
Home: Qualcomm Stadium, San Diego, California
World Series titles: 0
Fast fact: The team was owned for many years by McDonald's founder Ray Kroc.

SAN FRANCISCO GIANTS
Founded: 1883
Home: PacBell Park, San Francisco, California
World Series titles: 5
Fast fact: Team hasn't won a Series title since it moved from New York in 1958.

NATIONAL LEAGUE TEAMS ACROSS NORTH AMERICA

The World Series

THE WORLD SERIES IS PLAYED EACH fall between the champions of the American and National Leagues. The winner of the best-of-seven Series is the overall champion of Major League Baseball for that season. Four teams from each league earn berths in postseason playoffs that determine the two League champions. Because it has determined the best baseball team in the world every year since 1903, the World Series is, to many people, the touchstone by which baseball history is measured. The Fall Classic, as it is also known, has created baseball legends through heroic play and eternal goats through mistakes made in the international spotlight. For some teams, such as the New York Yankees, the World Series is an oft-visited place; for others, such as the Chicago Cubs or Boston Red Sox, a World Series championship is always "a year away." (For a list of World Series winners, see page 59.)

Giants' team logo

Diamond at center of ring

Year of championship

CHAMPIONSHIP RING
Each player on the World Series winning team, as well as the coaches and selected staff and front office personnel, receives a gold or silver ring encrusted with diamonds. A new ring is designed for each winning team. Willie Mays earned this ring with the Giants in 1954.

PROGRAMS
World Series programs are popular collectibles. They feature the team rosters and biographies, while more recent programs also include stories about World Series history.

Catcher Yogi Berra

Don Larsen

Official World Series logo for 1999

Logos of participants

Original name of event: World's Championship Games

Baseballs were premade for the Series that wasn't

THE YEAR OF NO SERIES
In 1994, the baseball season ended in August due to a labor dispute between players and owners. As a result, the World Series was not held that year for the first time since 1904.

PERFECT GAME
In Game 5 of the 1956 World Series, Yankee pitcher Don Larsen faced 27 Brooklyn Dodgers hitters... and recorded 27 consecutive outs. It was the only perfect game pitched in World Series play. The Yankees went on to win the Series in seven games.

MOST VALUABLE PLAYER
Following each World Series, media members choose the Series' Most Valuable Player. Scott Brosius of the Yankees accepts his award after the 1998 World Series.

Caps and T-shirts are made up in advance for the winners

World Series MVP Trophy

Television coverage has helped make the World Series popular around the world

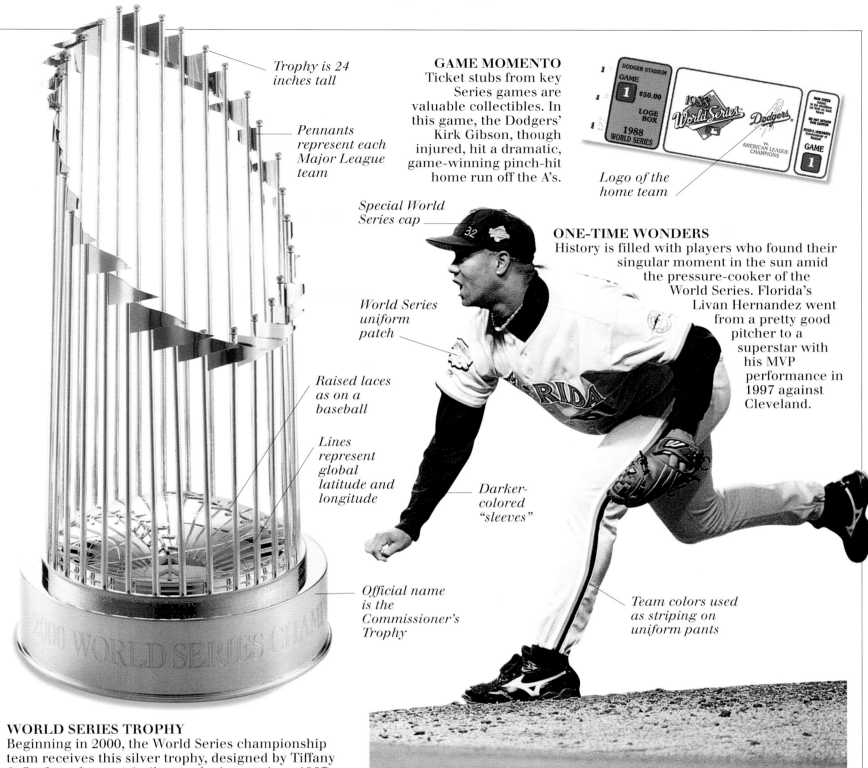

Trophy is 24 inches tall

Pennants represent each Major League team

GAME MOMENTO
Ticket stubs from key Series games are valuable collectibles. In this game, the Dodgers' Kirk Gibson, though injured, hit a dramatic, game-winning pinch-hit home run off the A's.

Logo of the home team

Special World Series cap

ONE-TIME WONDERS
History is filled with players who found their singular moment in the sun amid the pressure-cooker of the World Series. Florida's Livan Hernandez went from a pretty good pitcher to a superstar with his MVP performance in 1997 against Cleveland.

World Series uniform patch

Raised laces as on a baseball

Lines represent global latitude and longitude

Darker-colored "sleeves"

Official name is the Commissioner's Trophy

Team colors used as striping on uniform pants

WORLD SERIES TROPHY
Beginning in 2000, the World Series championship team receives this silver trophy, designed by Tiffany & Co. It replaces a similar trophy in use since 1967.

1999 MAJOR LEAGUE BASEBALL PLAYOFFS

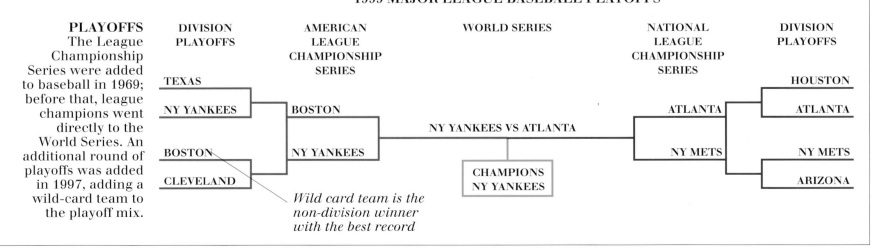

PLAYOFFS
The League Championship Series were added to baseball in 1969; before that, league champions went directly to the World Series. An additional round of playoffs was added in 1997, adding a wild-card team to the playoff mix.

DIVISION PLAYOFFS

AMERICAN LEAGUE CHAMPIONSHIP SERIES

WORLD SERIES

NATIONAL LEAGUE CHAMPIONSHIP SERIES

DIVISION PLAYOFFS

TEXAS
NY YANKEES
BOSTON
CLEVELAND

BOSTON
NY YANKEES

NY YANKEES VS ATLANTA

CHAMPIONS NY YANKEES

ATLANTA
NY METS

HOUSTON
ATLANTA
NY METS
ARIZONA

Wild card team is the non-division winner with the best record

The Baseball Hall of Fame

Each member of the Baseball Hall of Fame has a bronze plaque in a large wood-paneled room at the Hall. The plaque shows the player's face in bas-relief, along with a description of their career.

LOCATED IN COOPERSTOWN, New York, the Baseball Hall of Fame and Museum (below) is the repository of the game's history and the place of honor for the greatest players and contributors to the sport. The first group of members of the Hall was elected in 1936; a building to house the exhibits, memorabilia, a baseball research library, and the Hall of Fame Gallery was dedicated in 1939. New members of the Hall of Fame are chosen annually by the Baseball Writers of America. Players must be retired five years to be eligible. Other people who can be elected to the Hall include managers, umpires, team executives, and broadcasters. A special Veterans' Committee also can select a player from baseball's distant past who was overlooked in past voting. Each August, a ceremony is held at which the new members are enshrined. The spreading lawn beside the Hall fills with thousands of fans, there to watch another page of baseball history being written.

Players who have been on more than one team can choose the baseball cap they're shown wearing

Each player is framed by carved greenery and a baseball motif

GEORGE HOWARD BRETT
KANSAS CITY, A.L., 1973 – 1993

PLAYED EACH GAME WITH CEASELESS INTENSITY AND UNBRIDLED PASSION LIFETIME MARKS INCLUDE .305 BA, 317 HR, 1,595 RBI AND 3,154 HITS ELEVEN .300 SEASONS. A 13-TIME ALL-STAR AND THE FIRST PLAYER TO WIN BATTING TITLES IN THREE DECADES (1976, '80, '90). HIT .390 IN 1980 MVP SEASON AND LED ROYALS TO FIRST WORLD SERIES TITLE IN 1985. RANKS AMONG ALL-TIME LEADERS IN HITS, DOUBLES, LONG HITS AND TOTAL BASES. A.L. CAREER RECORD, MOST INTENTIONAL WALKS. A CLUTCH HITTER WHOSE PROFOUND RESPECT FOR THE GAME LED TO UNIVERSAL REVERENCE.

Player name, dates of play

THE BASEBALL HALL OF FAME

Details of player's career, featuring records and skills

HISTORY ON DISPLAY
These large cabinets are typical of the displays at the Hall of Fame. They include photographs, uniforms, descriptive copy, and memorabilia.

PRIDE AND PASSION
THE AFRICAN AMERICAN BASEBALL EXPERIENCE

SPECIAL EXHIBITS
This exhibit on the varied and often troubling story of blacks in baseball highlights the Hall's ability to show a complete picture of baseball history, warts and all. Photos, uniforms, memorabilia, and more were included.

BASEBALLS
The Hall has an enormous collection of baseballs used in the game's most important moments. Players usually are pleased to present their momentos to the Hall for posterity. This ball is from Nolan Ryan's record seventh no-hitter.

FAMOUS GEAR

Brooklyn Dodgers logo

Hats in Robinson's time were made of wool

JACKIE ROBINSON'S HAT
This hat, worn by Jackie Robinson, is one of thousands of pieces of gear from more than 100 years of baseball collected and displayed by the Hall.

BASEBALL THEATER
From early shorts to recordings of the poem *Casey at the Bat* to modern features like *Bull Durham* and *Eight Men Out*, baseball has long been a subject of films. This exhibit at the Hall celebrates baseball movies and features memorabilia from a century of films.

Classic Yankee pinstripes

JOE DIMAGGIO'S JERSEY
One of the great hallmarks of the artifacts fans can see at the Hall of Fame is their authenticity. This jersey, worn by Yankee great Joe DiMaggio, still has the sweat, dirt, and grass stains that the "Yankee Clipper" put there himself.

Honus Wagner · Grover Cleveland Alexander · Tris Speaker · Napoleon Lajoie · George Sisler · Walter Johnson

Eddie Collins · Babe Ruth · Connie Mack · Cy Young

GATHERING OF GREATS
In this 1939 photo, all the living members of the Baseball Hall of Fame were present at the Hall's dedication. Ty Cobb also was at the event, but missed being in this photograph. All were players, except longtime Philadelphia manager Connie Mack.

Baseball cards

ALTHOUGH THEY ARE LITTLE MORE THAN rectangles of cardboard printed on both sides with pictures and numbers, baseball cards have come to symbolize many things to fans. Pro players first began appearing on cards in cigarette and tobacco packages in the 1870s – among the first uses of sports figures in advertisements. To fans of the early game in the days before television, the colorful cards were the way they could see the heroes they otherwise only read about. For many ensuing decades, baseball cards were the province of kids, who traded and collected them worshipfully. In the 1970s and 1980s, these former child's trinkets skyrocketed in value, with rare cards fetching hundreds of thousands of dollars. The craze has died out a bit, but baseball cards remain a big business. And while every sport today has trading cards, baseball had them first.

CHRISTY MATHEWSON CARD, 1900s

Hand-colored black and white photo

Player's signature

BARRIER BREAKER
In 1947, Jackie Robinson became the first African-American in the 20th century to play in the Major Leagues. By breaking baseball's color line, he became an international hero. This card lists him as an outfielder – a position he rarely played.

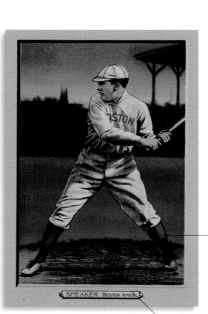

Printing technology didn't allow for mass production of color photos

HANDPAINTED CARD, 1880s

Tris Speaker name panel

Note early spelling of Pittsburgh without final "h"

Niekro was noted for successfully throwing knuckleballs

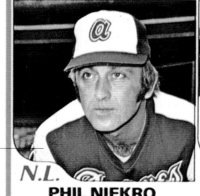

RAREST CIGARETTE CARD
Only a handful of this 1910 Honus Wagner card are known to exist. The abstemious Wagner objected to a tobacco company using him on this card, and it was removed from circulation. The few cards that slipped through have become the most valuable on the market, fetching prices in excess of $500,000 for cards in very good condition.

"TWO-FER" CARD

Ryan became the all-time strikeout leader

PACK OF CARDS
Until the 1990s, packs of baseball cards contained a stick of chewing gum, but the tradition was ended to protect cards for collectors.

ON THE BACK
On the back side, baseball cards are filled with the featured player's complete Major League statistical record.

Card number, to aid collectors of entire sets

Vital statistics

Player photo

Player's position

Statistical categories

Year-by-year career statistics

Annual totals in a variety of categories

Team played on

Career notes

Career totals

Holographic background

Card company logo

Seal of authenticity

Major League Baseball logo

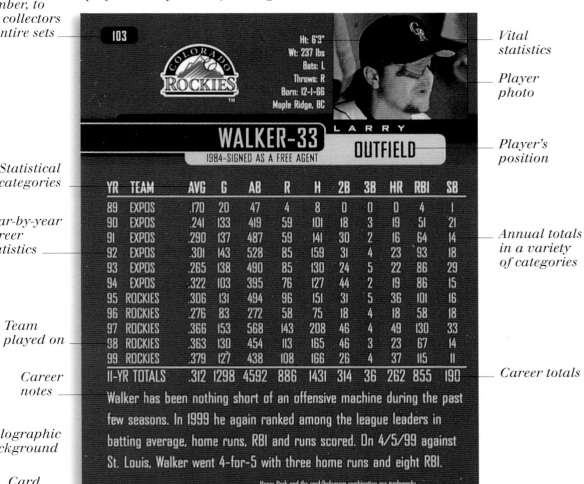

103

Ht: 6'3"
Wt: 237 lbs
Bats: L
Throws: R
Born: 12-1-66
Maple Ridge, BC

WALKER-33
1984—SIGNED AS A FREE AGENT

LARRY
OUTFIELD

YR	TEAM	AVG	G	AB	R	H	2B	3B	HR	RBI	SB
89	EXPOS	.170	20	47	4	8	0	0	0	4	1
90	EXPOS	.241	133	419	59	101	18	3	19	51	21
91	EXPOS	.290	137	487	59	141	30	2	16	64	14
92	EXPOS	.301	143	528	85	159	31	4	23	93	18
93	EXPOS	.265	138	490	85	130	24	5	22	86	29
94	EXPOS	.322	103	395	76	127	44	2	19	86	15
95	ROCKIES	.306	131	494	96	151	31	5	36	101	16
96	ROCKIES	.276	83	272	58	75	18	4	18	58	18
97	ROCKIES	.366	153	568	143	208	46	4	49	130	33
98	ROCKIES	.363	130	454	113	165	46	3	23	67	14
99	ROCKIES	.379	127	438	108	166	26	4	37	115	11
11-YR TOTALS		.312	1298	4592	886	1431	314	36	262	855	190

Walker has been nothing short of an offensive machine during the past few seasons. In 1999 he again ranked among the league leaders in batting average, home runs, RBI and runs scored. On 4/5/99 against St. Louis, Walker went 4-for-5 with three home runs and eight RBI.

Upper Deck and the card/hologram combination are trademarks of The Upper Deck Company, LLC. ©1999 The Upper Deck Company, LLC. All Rights Reserved. Printed in the U.S.A. Major League Baseball trademarks and copyrights are used with permission of Major League Baseball Properties, Inc. ©MLBPA Official Licensee of Major League Baseball Players Association.

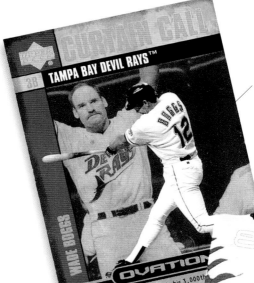

TAMPA BAY DEVIL RAYS™

8/7/99: Boggs collects his 3,000th

FANCY CARDS
To create cards that stand out in an increasingly crowded market, companies today use a variety of exotic printing techniques.

Embossed with baseball-like red stitching

Cal Ripken Jr. #8

National League logo

American League logo

FENWAY PARK™
1912
ALL-STAR GAME '99
BOSTON ☆ JULY 13

CELEBRATION CARDS
Cards are issued to note special events, such as this one of Fenway Park from the 1999 All-Star Game.

Other baseball leagues

ORGANIZED BASEBALL IS PLAYED, AND HAS been played, at many levels alongside the Major Leagues since professional baseball began. One of the most prominent was the Negro Leagues, which came into being before World War I when the Major Leagues banned African-Americans from joining their teams. Until the color barrier fell when Jackie Robinson joined the Brooklyn Dodgers in 1947, thousands of talented black baseball players found an outlet for their skills in the Negro Leagues. Women, too, were excluded from the pros, until a shortage of men in World War II led to the formation of the All-American Girls' Professional Baseball League. But after the war ended, male players returned, and the league disbanded in 1954. The minor leagues are perhaps the most important other baseball organization. Hundreds of teams, most affiliated with Major League clubs, act as incubators of young talent. The minors have been a part of many smaller American towns and cities for a century.

JOSH GIBSON
Dubbed the "Black Babe Ruth" for his powerful swing, Gibson batted over .350 for 17 seasons, hit an estimated 950 home runs, and led the Homestead Grays to nine Negro League pennants. He was elected to the Baseball Hall of Fame in 1972.

WOMEN IN ACTION
As this play shows, the action in the AAGBL was just as furious as in the men's pro leagues. But after World War II, interest in women's baseball died out.

PENNANT FROM AAGBL PEORIA REDWINGS

PEORIA ILL.

SATCHEL PAIGE
One of the most enthusiastic players ever, Paige starred for several Negro League teams before finally joining the Cleveland Indians as a 42-year-old rookie in 1948. He, too, is in the Hall of Fame.

In offseason exhibitions, Paige would tell the fielders to sit down and then strike out the other side

AAGBL players wore skirts over shorts

NEGRO LEAGUE BIRMINGHAM BLACK BARONS CAP

Knee socks

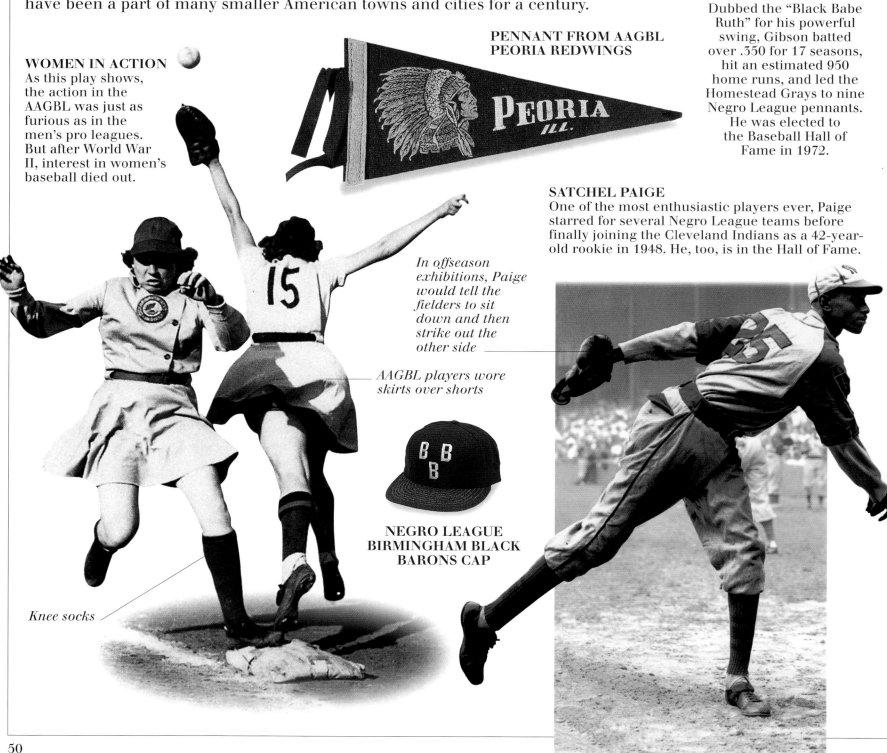

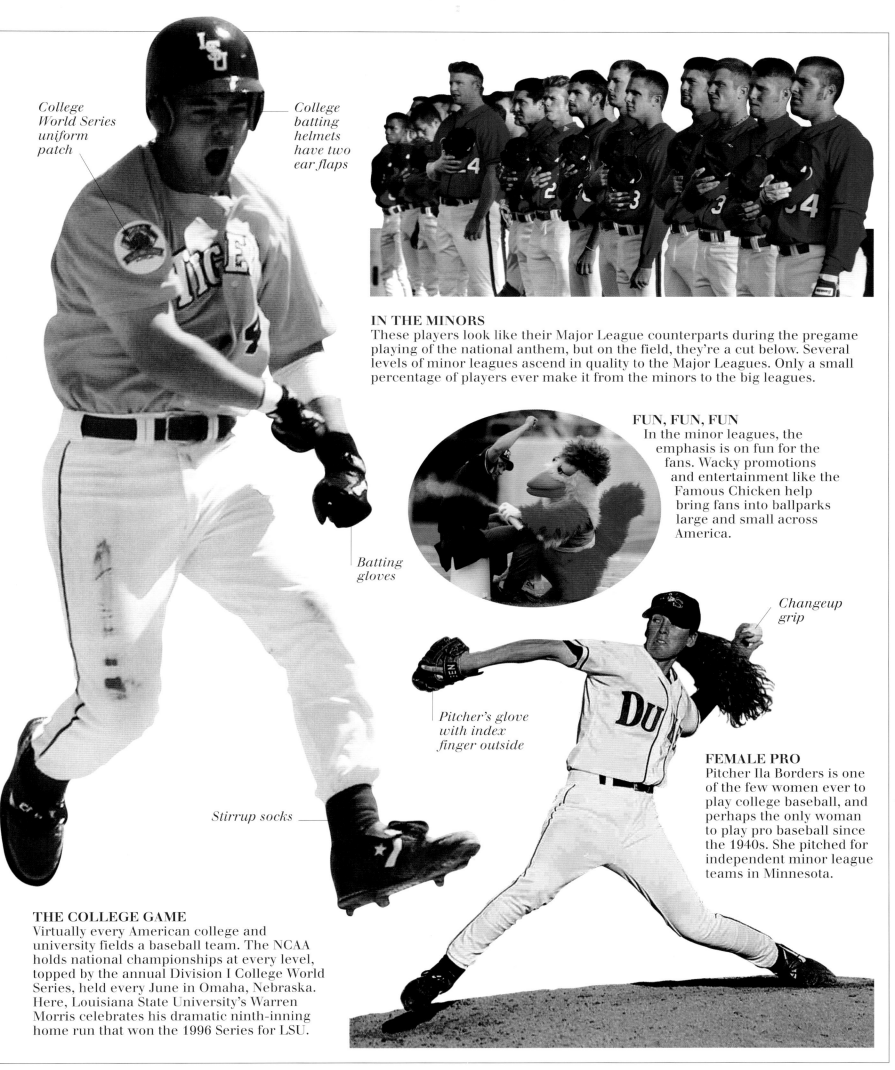

College World Series uniform patch

College batting helmets have two ear flaps

Batting gloves

Stirrup socks

IN THE MINORS

These players look like their Major League counterparts during the pregame playing of the national anthem, but on the field, they're a cut below. Several levels of minor leagues ascend in quality to the Major Leagues. Only a small percentage of players ever make it from the minors to the big leagues.

FUN, FUN, FUN

In the minor leagues, the emphasis is on fun for the fans. Wacky promotions and entertainment like the Famous Chicken help bring fans into ballparks large and small across America.

Changeup grip

Pitcher's glove with index finger outside

FEMALE PRO

Pitcher Ila Borders is one of the few women ever to play college baseball, and perhaps the only woman to play pro baseball since the 1940s. She pitched for independent minor league teams in Minnesota.

THE COLLEGE GAME

Virtually every American college and university fields a baseball team. The NCAA holds national championships at every level, topped by the annual Division I College World Series, held every June in Omaha, Nebraska. Here, Louisiana State University's Warren Morris celebrates his dramatic ninth-inning home run that won the 1996 Series for LSU.

Youth baseball

WHETHER IN ORGANIZED LEAGUES or in parks, sandlots, or streets around the world, millions of kids play baseball. The sport is consistently ranked among the most popular in polls of youngsters, with many girls joining boys in recent years to help swell the ranks of young players. Many kids play in organized leagues under the guidance of coaches, using uniforms and equipment just like their Major League heroes. Little League Baseball, Inc., is the largest youth baseball organization in the world, with baseball and softball leagues in 82 countries for nearly three million boys and girls ages eight to 15. Other major American youth baseball organizations include Dixie Baseball, Babe Ruth Baseball, and PONY Baseball. All of these leagues strive to teach sportsmanship, teamwork, and, of course, baseball skills. Kids today are part of a continuum of young people who constantly refresh the game, bringing the enthusiasm of discovery to a game that keeps people who stay involved with it forever young.

LEARN FROM THE PROS
Whether at a clinic with Baltimore Orioles great Cal Ripken, Jr., or just by watching on television, kids learn about baseball skills by watching Major Leaguers.

Protective throat guard flap

Face mask with attached helmet

Youth catcher's mitt

Chest protector covers groin area

Shin guards with knee protection

Uniforms in tee ball are often T-shirts

Adjustable rubber and plastic tee

TEE BALL
A popular way for younger players to get started is in tee ball. Instead of batting against a pitcher, players use a regular baseball bat to hit the ball from a plastic tee. This enables them to learn the basic batting stroke and practice fielding and baserunning without the pressure of facing a pitcher.

Padded outfield fence, about 200 feet from home

Scoreboard

LITTLE LEAGUE FIELD
Youth fields are normally smaller than adult fields. As players get older, the base paths they use get longer.

60-foot basepath

Catcher's and umpire's boxes

YOUNG CATCHER
Safety is important in organized youth leagues. Equipment is carefully selected to protect young players. Like their Major League counterparts, catchers are well-protected by pads.

Labeled as approved for youth play

Manufacturer's logo

Ear flap with ventilation hole

Chin strap

YOUNG CHAMPS
Japan won the 1999 Little League World Series, an annual international championship held in Williamsport, Pennsylvania, since 1954.

SWINGING METAL
Most youth leagues use aluminum bats instead of wood. These bats are lighter weight and much more durable than wood, thus making them more cost-efficient.

Far East is one of eight regions at the Little League World Series

Deep, flexible webbing

Rubber grip

Deep, premade central pocket

YOUTH GLOVE
Baseball gloves for younger players are very similar to those for adults. Shorter fingers make them easier to wear, while deeper pockets make learning to catch easier.

Soft, flexible heel

PINS TO TRADE
Pin trading is an internationally popular hobby. Teams, leagues, nations, companies, and more make pins that fans collect and trade.

KIDS IN JAPAN
Youth baseball is not limited to the United States. As these young Japanese fans attest, the game is popular with fans and players of all ages around the world.

53

Softball games

SOFTBALL IS THE MOST POPULAR derivative of baseball. The game, played very much like baseball, uses a larger, softer ball in both fast-pitch and slow-pitch varieties. It was created in 1887 when George Hancock used an old boxing glove to play a game he first called "indoor-outdoor baseball." Rules for the game were codified, and today slow-pitch softball is one of the most popular recreation sports in America and is played around the world. The fast-pitch version is played at competitive levels up to the Olympics, primarily by female players. Chicagoans play a unique version of the game using a softer, 16-inch ball. Children have developed several varieties of baseball, adapting the bat-and-ball basics to their own situations. New York City streets, for instance, gave birth to stickball, played with broomsticks and small rubber balls.

SOFTBALL
Softballs measure 12 inches in circumference and weigh between 6¼ and 7 ounces.

STICKBALL
This city street version of baseball is played with thin bats and deadened tennis balls. Varities include fast-pitch and one-bounce.

FAST-PITCH SOFTBALL
This version of softball is played primarily by women at all levels, including the Olympics. Pitchers stand 40 feet from home plate and must pitch from inside a 10-foot diameter circle. The windmill windup of top pitchers can generate pitch speeds approaching 80 mph.

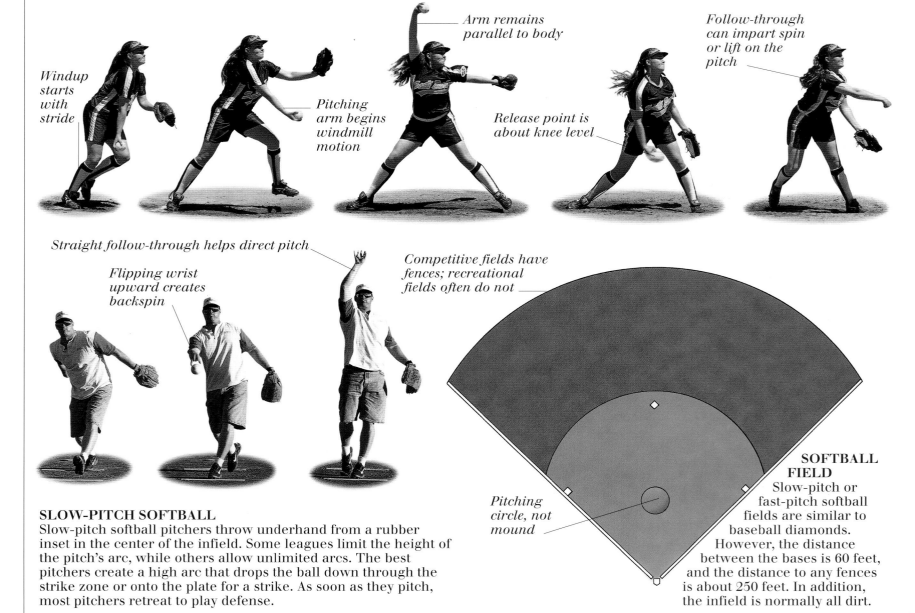

Windup starts with stride

Pitching arm begins windmill motion

Arm remains parallel to body

Release point is about knee level

Follow-through can impart spin or lift on the pitch

Straight follow-through helps direct pitch

Flipping wrist upward creates backspin

Competitive fields have fences; recreational fields often do not

Pitching circle, not mound

SOFTBALL FIELD
Slow-pitch or fast-pitch softball fields are similar to baseball diamonds. However, the distance between the bases is 60 feet, and the distance to any fences is about 250 feet. In addition, the infield is normally all dirt.

SLOW-PITCH SOFTBALL
Slow-pitch softball pitchers throw underhand from a rubber inset in the center of the infield. Some leagues limit the height of the pitch's arc, while others allow unlimited arcs. The best pitchers create a high arc that drops the ball down through the strike zone or onto the plate for a strike. As soon as they pitch, most pitchers retreat to play defense.

SOFT PITCH
In Over-the-Line, teammates pitch to one another with a soft lob toss.

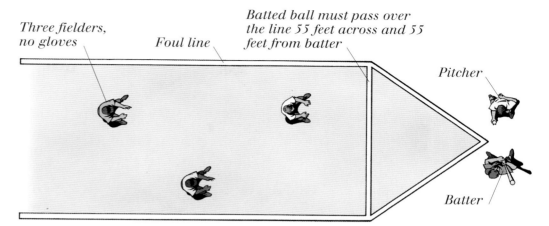

Three fielders, no gloves

Foul line

Batted ball must pass over the line 55 feet across and 55 feet from batter

Pitcher

Batter

OVER-THE-LINE
This unique form of softball was created in 1954 by a group of bored volleyball players in San Diego, California. Batters try to place hits among three opposing fielders. There is no baserunning; hits are assigned "bases" based on distance. While it can be played anywhere, this is traditionally a beach game.

FAST-PITCH BATTING
The short distance between pitcher and batter in fast-pitch softball means that batters must react especially quickly. Some pitchers are so hard to hit that most players simply try to bunt their way on; it's not unusual to see third basemen playing very close to home plate to stop this ploy.

Aluminum softball bat

SLOW-PITCH BATTING
Slow-pitch batters must learn to time the arc of the pitch so that their bat meets the ball at just the right moment.

Catcher wears face mask, chest protector, and shin guards

Women's softball teams usually wear short pants

High knee socks help protect legs while sliding

Baseball around the world

ALTHOUGH IT'S CALLED AMERICA'S National Pastime, baseball is played in more than 100 countries around the world. From its beginnings in the northeastern United States in the 1850s, baseball moved first to Canada and then south of the border. The game caught on quickly in Mexico, Venezuela, and Spanish-speaking Caribbean nations such as Cuba, which became the site of a popular winter league that included American stars. Today, the island nation of the Dominican Republic sends more players to the Major Leagues than any country outside the U.S. American soldiers also brought the game with them on foreign tours of duty. As a result, after World War II a nascent baseball movement in Japan blossomed, and today it has the second-biggest professional league in the world. With youth leagues growing around the world and Major League Baseball organizing international tours, the sport's expansion continues.

Japanese pro leagues use wood bats

Batting helmet printed with team slogan or player's name

Satoshi Nakajima of the Seibu Lions

OLYMPIC BASEBALL
Baseball was a demonstration sport at several Summer Olympic Games before gaining full medal status in 1992. Teams from Europe, Asia, and the Americas have taken part, but Cuba has dominated the competition.

BASEBALL IN JAPAN
Baseball has been played in Japan since the late 1800s. A pro league was formed in 1936; today it is made up of the Central and Pacific Leagues, with six teams each. American players can be found on Japanese teams, and a few Japanese players have come to the U.S.

Players in blue from the Netherlands

Sliding player from Australia, a country that also has a professional baseball league

Plastic guard protects foot and ankle from foul tips

PROS ON TOUR

Mike Piazza of the New York Mets was greeted at Japan's Tokyo Dome in May 2000, where the Mets and the Chicago Cubs played the first regular-season game ever held outside the United States or Canada. The game was part of Major League Baseball's drive to promote the sport worldwide.

Piazza followed in the footsteps of pros who started visiting Japan to play in the 1920s

Mexico is one of many countries that play baseball in the Pan Am Games

EL BÉISBOL

Baseball is immensely popular in Latin America, especially in Mexico, Venezuela, and the Dominican Republic. These countries are sending an increasing number of players to the U.S. Major Leagues.

THE GIANTS

The dominant team in Japanese baseball has been the Tokyo Yomiuri Giants, who have won 17 titles since the Japan Series began in 1950. This newspaper celebrates a moment from a recent season.

Fidel Castro in 1962

BASEBALL IN CUBA

The best teams in international competition often come from Cuba, home of a professional league and a long record of excellence. Baseball is enormously popular there, inspired partly by Fidel Castro's great love of the game. The future Cuban leader once tried out as a pitcher for the New York Yankees.

The uniform of jersey, knee-length pants and stirrup socks is used worldwide

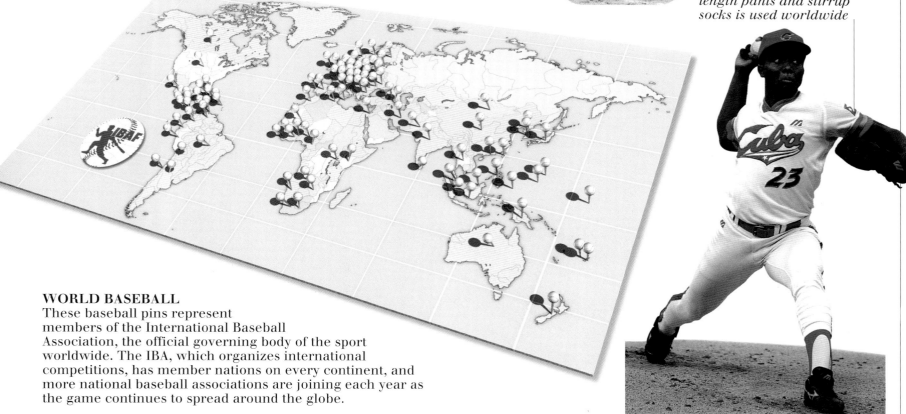

WORLD BASEBALL

These baseball pins represent members of the International Baseball Association, the official governing body of the sport worldwide. The IBA, which organizes international competitions, has member nations on every continent, and more national baseball associations are joining each year as the game continues to spread around the globe.

Appendix

All-Time Top 10

The best career records in major categories through 1999.

PITCHING

EARNED RUN AVERAGE		WINS		STRIKEOUTS		SAVES	
Ed Walsh	1.80	Cy Young	511	Nolan Ryan	5,714	Lee Smith	478
Addie Joss	1.89	Walter Johnson	417	Steve Carlton	4,136	John Franco	416
Mordecai Brown	2.06	Pete Alexander	373	Bert Blyleven	3,701	Dennis Eckersley	390
John Ward	2.10	Christy Mathewson	373	Tom Seaver	3,640	Jeff Reardon	367
Christy Mathewson	2.13	Warren Spahn	363	Don Sutton	3,574	Randy Myers	347
Rube Waddell	2.16	Jim Galvin	361	Gaylord Perry	3,534	Rollie Fingers	341
Walter Johnson	2.17	Kid Nichols	361	Walter Johnson	3,509	Tom Henke	311
Orval Overall	2.23	Tim Keefe	342	Phil Niekro	3,342	Rich Gossage	310
Tommy Bond	2.25	Steve Carlton	329	Roger Clemens	3,316	Bruce Sutter	300
Ed Reulbach	2.28	John Clarkson	328	Ferguson Jenkins	3,192	Jeff Montgomery	292
Will White	2.28						

BATTING

HITS		HOME RUNS		RUNS BATTED IN		BATTING AVERAGE		STOLEN BASES	
Pete Rose	4,256	Hank Aaron	755	Hank Aaron	2,297	Ty Cobb	.366	Rickey Henderson	1,344
Ty Cobb	4,189	Babe Ruth	714	Babe Ruth	2,213	Rogers Hornsby	.358	Lou Brock	938
Hank Aaron	3,771	Willie Mays	660	Lou Gehrig	1,995	Joe Jackson	.356	Billy Hamilton	912
Stan Musial	3,630	Frank Robinson	586	Stan Musial	1,951	Ed Delahanty	.346	Ty Cobb	892
Tris Speaker	3,514	Harmon Killebrew	573	Ty Cobb	1,937	Tris Speaker	.345	Tim Raines	807
Carl Yastrzemski	3,419	Reggie Jackson	563	Jimmie Foxx	1,922	Ted Williams	.344	Vince Coleman	752
Honus Wagner	3,415	Mike Schmidt	548	Eddie Murray	1,917	Billy Hamilton	.344	Eddie Collins	744
Paul Molitor	3,319	Mickey Mantle	536	Willie Mays	1,903	Dan Brouthers	.344	Arlie Latham	739
Eddie Collins	3,315	Jimmie Foxx	534	Cap Anson	1,879	Babe Ruth	.342	Max Carey	738
Willie Mays	3,283	Mark McGwire	522	Mel Ott	1,860	Harry Heilmann	.342	Honus Wagner	722

Hank Aaron

Triple Crown Winners

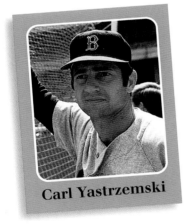

Carl Yastrzemski

A batter who leads the league in home runs, runs batted in, and batting average in one season is the winner of the Triple Crown. It had been accomplished only 16 times through the 1999 season, most recently in 1967.

YEAR	PLAYER, TEAM (LEAGUE)	Year	PLAYER, TEAM (LEAGUE)
1878	Paul Hines, Providence (NL)	1933	Chuck Klein, Philadelphia (NL)
1894	Hugh Duffy, Boston (NL)	1934	Lou Gehrig, New York (AL)
1901	Napoleon Lajoie, Philadelphia (AL)	1937	Joe Medwick, St. Louis (NL)
1909	Ty Cobb, Detroit (AL)	1942	Ted Williams, Boston (AL)
1912	Heinie Zimmerman, Chicago (NL)	1947	Ted Williams, Boston (AL)
1922	Rogers Hornsby, St. Louis (NL)	1956	Mickey Mantle, New York (AL)
1925	Rogers Hornsby, St. Louis (NL)	1966	Frank Robinson, Baltimore (AL)
1933	Jimmie Foxx, Philadelphia (AL)	1967	Carl Yastrzemski, Boston (AL)

Single-Season Record Holders

Best single-season marks since 1900 through the 1999 season.

HITS	RUNS BATTED IN	WINS
257, George Sisler, 1920	190, Hack Wilson, 1930	41, Jack Chesbro, 1904
HOME RUNS	**BATTING AVERAGE**	**ERA**
70, Mark McGwire, 1998	.426, Napoleon Lajoie, 1901	0.96, Dutch Leonard, 1914
TOTAL BASES	**STOLEN BASES**	**SAVES**
457, Babe Ruth, 1921	130, Rickey Henderson, 1982	57, Bobby Thigpen, 1990

Mark McGwire

World Series Champions

1999 New York (AL) 4, Atlanta (NL) 0	1966 Baltimore (AL) 4, Los Angeles (NL) 0	1933 New York (NL) 4, Washington (AL) 1
1998 New York (AL) 4, San Diego (NL) 0	1965 Los Angeles (NL) 4, Minnesota (AL) 3	1932 New York (AL) 4, Chicago (NL) 0
1997 Florida (NL) 4, Cleveland (AL) 3	1964 St.Louis (NL) 4, New York (AL) 3	1931 St. Louis (NL) 4, Philadelphia (AL) 3
1996 New York (AL) 4, Atlanta (NL) 2	1963 Los Angeles (NL) 4, New York (AL) 0	1930 Philadelphia (AL) 4, St. Louis (NL) 2
1995 Atlanta (NL) 4, Cleveland (AL) 2	1962 New York (AL) 4, San Francisco (NL) 3	1929 Philadelphia (AL) 4, Chicago (NL) 1
1994 No series due to players strike	1961 New York (AL) 4, Cincinnati (NL) 1	1928 New York (AL) 4, St. Louis (NL) 0
1993 Toronto (AL) 4, Philadelphia (NL) 2	1960 Pittsburgh (NL) 4, New York (AL) 3	1927 New York (AL) 4, Pittsburgh (NL) 0
1992 Toronto (AL) 4, Atlanta (NL) 2	1959 Los Angeles (NL) 4, Chicago (AL) 2	1926 St. Louis (NL) 4, New York (AL) 3
1991 Minnesota (AL) 4, Atlanta (NL) 3	1958 New York (AL) 4, Milwaukee (NL) 3	1925 Pittsburgh (NL) 4, Washington (AL) 3
1990 Cincinnati (NL) 4, Oakland (AL) 0	1957 Milwaukee (NL) 4, New York (AL) 3	1924 Washington (AL) 4, New York (NL) 3
1989 Oakland (AL) 4, San Francisco (NL) 0	1956 New York (AL) 4, Brooklyn (NL) 3	1923 New York (AL) 4, New York (NL) 2
1988 Los Angeles (NL) 4, Oakland (AL) 1	1955 Brooklyn (NL) 4, New York (AL) 3	1922 New York (NL) 4, New York (AL) 0, 1 tie
1987 Minnesota (AL) 4, St. Louis (NL) 3	1954 New York (NL) 4, Cleveland (AL) 0	1921 New York (NL) 5, New York (AL) 3
1986 New York (NL) 4, Boston (AL) 3	1953 New York (AL) 4, Brooklyn (NL) 2	1920 Cleveland (AL) 5, Brooklyn (NL) 2
1985 Kansas City (AL) 4, St. Louis (NL) 3	1952 New York (AL) 4, Brooklyn (NL) 3	1919 Cincinnati (NL) 5, Chicago (AL) 3
1984 Detroit (AL) 4, San Diego (NL) 1	1951 New York (AL) 4, New York (NL) 2	1918 Boston (AL) 4, Chicago (NL) 2
1983 Baltimore (AL) 4, Philadelphia (NL) 1	1950 New York (AL) 4, Philadelphia (NL) 0	1917 Chicago (AL) 4, New York (NL) 2
1982 St. Louis (NL) 4, Milwaukee (AL) 3	1949 New York (AL) 4, Brooklyn (NL) 1	1916 Boston (AL) 4, Brooklyn (NL) 1
1981 Los Angeles (NL) 4, New York (AL) 2	1948 Cleveland (AL) 4, Boston (NL) 2	1915 Boston (AL) 4, Philadelphia (NL) 1
1980 Philadelphia (NL) 4, Kansas City (AL) 2	1947 New York (AL) 4, Brooklyn (NL) 3	1914 Boston (NL) 4, Philadelphia (AL) 0
1979 Pittsburgh (NL) 4, Baltimore (AL) 3	1946 St. Louis (NL) 4, Boston (AL) 3	1913 Philadelphia (AL) 4, New York (NL) 1
1978 New York (AL) 4, Los Angeles (NL) 2	1945 Detroit (AL) 4, Chicago (NL) 3	1912 Boston (AL) 4, New York (NL) 3, 1 tie
1977 New York (AL) 4, Los Angeles (NL) 2	1944 St. Louis (NL) 4, St. Louis (AL) 2	1911 Philadelphia (AL) 4, New York (NL) 2
1976 Cincinnati (NL) 4, New York (AL) 0	1943 New York (AL) 4, St. Louis (NL) 1	1910 Philadelphia (AL) 4, Chicago (NL) 1
1975 Cincinnati (NL) 4, Boston (AL) 3	1942 St. Louis (NL) 4, New York (AL) 1	1909 Pittsburgh (NL) 4, Detroit (AL) 3
1974 Oakland (AL) 4, Los Angeles (NL) 1	1941 New York (AL) 4, Brooklyn (NL) 1	1908 Chicago (NL) 4, Detroit (AL) 1
1973 Oakland (AL) 4, New York (NL) 3	1940 Cincinnati (NL) 4, Detroit (AL) 3	1907 Chicago (NL) 4, Detroit (AL) 0, one tie
1972 Oakland (AL) 4, Cincinnati (NL) 3	1939 New York (AL) 4, Cincinnati (NL) 0	1906 Chicago (AL) 4, Chicago (NL) 2
1971 Pittsburgh (NL) 4, Baltimore (AL) 3	1938 New York (AL) 4, Chicago (NL) 0	1905 New York (NL) 4, Philadelphia (AL) 1
1970 Baltimore (AL) 4, Cincinnati (NL) 1	1937 New York (AL) 4, New York (NL) 1	1904 no series
1969 New York (NL) 4, Baltimore (AL) 1	1936 New York (AL) 4, New York (NL) 2	1903 Boston (AL) 5, Pittsburgh (NL) 3
1968 Detroit (AL) 4, St. Louis (NL) 3	1935 Detroit (AL) 4, Chicago (NL) 2	
1967 St. Louis (NL) 4, Boston (AL) 3	1934 St. Louis (NL) 4, Detroit (AL) 3	

NL: National League; AL: American League
Note: In 1903 and 1919-21, the World Series was the best of nine games. All others are best of seven.

Perfect Games

A pitcher who retires all 27 players he faces without allowing a runner on base by any means (hit, error, hit batter, etc.) has pitched one of baseball's rarities: a perfect game. A perfect game differs from a no-hitter, in which a pitcher gives up no hits but allows men on base via walks, errors, or other means.

J.L. Richmond, 1880
J.M. Ward, 1880
Cy Young, 1904
Addie Joss, 1908
Charlie Robertson, 1922
Don Larsen, 1956*
Jim Bunning, 1964
Sandy Koufax, 1965
Catfish Hunter, 1968
Len Barker, 1981
Mike Witt, 1984
Tom Browning, 1988
Terry Mulholland, 1990
Dennis Martinez, 1991
Kenny Rogers, 1994
David Wells, 1998
David Cone, 1999

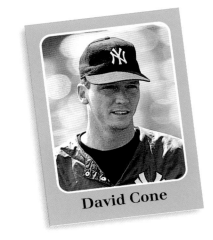
David Cone

* Only perfect game in the World Series

Super Streaks

Two types of streak are closely followed in baseball. Cal Ripken, Jr.'s, record for consecutive games played seems invincible; but then again, so did Lou "The Iron Horse" Gehrig's mark until Ripken bested it in 1996. Similarly, Joe DiMaggio's 56-game hitting streak (a safe hit in each of 56 consecutive games) continues to seem insurmountable, although several players have made attempts.

TOP FIVE CONSECUTIVE GAMES PLAYED STREAKS

Cal Ripken, Jr.	2,632
Lou Gehrig	2,130
Everett Scott	1,307
Steve Garvey	1,207
Billy Williams	1,117

TOP FIVE HITTING STREAKS

Joe DiMaggio, 1941	56 games
Willie Keeler, 1897	44 games
Pete Rose, 1978	44 games
Bill Dahlen, 1894	42 games
George Sisler, 1922	41 games

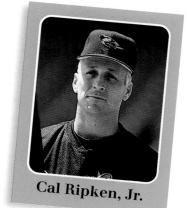
Cal Ripken, Jr.

Major League Baseball All-Century Team

Selected in 1999 by a national poll of fans, listed by position in order of votes received (*additional players added by a Major League Baseball select panel).

CATCHERS
Johnny Bench, Cincinnati Reds 1967-83
Yogi Berra, New York Yankees 1946-65

FIRST BASEMEN
Lou Gehrig, New York Yankees 1923-39
Mark McGwire, Oakland Athletics 1986-97, St. Louis Cardinals 1997-

SECOND BASEMEN
Jackie Robinson, Brooklyn Dodgers 1947-1956
Rogers Hornsby, St. Louis Cardinals 1915-26, New York Giants 1927, Boston Braves 1928, Chicago Cubs 1929-32, St. Louis Browns 1933-37

SHORTSTOPS
Cal Ripken, Jr., Baltimore Orioles 1982-
Ernie Banks, Chicago Cubs 1953-71
*Honus Wagner, Louisville Colonels 1897-99, Pittsburgh Pirates 1900-17

THIRD BASEMEN
Mike Schmidt, Philadelphia Phillies 1972-89
Brooks Robinson, Baltimore Orioles 1955-77

OUTFIELDERS
Babe Ruth, Boston Red Sox 1914-19, N.Y. Yankees 1920-34, Boston Braves 1935

Ken Griffey, Jr.

Hank Aaron, Milwaukee/Atlanta Braves 1954-74, Milwaukee Brewers 1975-76
Ted Williams, Boston Red Sox 1939-60
Willie Mays, New York/San Francisco Giants 1951-72, New York Mets 1972-73
Joe DiMaggio, New York Yankees 1936-51
Mickey Mantle, NewYork Yankees 1951-68
Ty Cobb, Detroit Tigers 1905-26, Philadelphia Athletics 1927-28
Ken Griffey, Jr., Seattle Mariners 1989-99, Cincinnati Reds 2000-
Pete Rose, Cincinnati Reds 1963-78 and 1984-86, Philadelphia Phillies 1979-83, Montreal Expos 1984
*Stan Musial, St. Louis Cardinals 1941-63

PITCHERS
Nolan Ryan, New York Mets 1966-71, California Angels 1972-79, Houston Astros 1980-88, Texas Rangers 1990-93
Sandy Koufax, Brooklyn/Los Angeles Dodgers 1955-66
Cy Young, Cleveland Spiders 1890-98, St. Louis Cardinals 1899-1900, Boston Pilgrims/Red Sox 1901-08, Cleveland Indians 1909-11, Boston Braves 1911
Roger Clemens, Boston Red Sox 1984-96, Toronto Blue Jays 1997-98, New York Yankees 1999-
Bob Gibson, St. Louis Cardinals 1959-75
Walter Johnson, Washington Senators 1907-27
*Warren Spahn, Boston/Milwaukee Braves 1942-65, New York Mets 1965, San Francisco Giants 1965
*Lefty Grove, Philadelphia Athletics 1925-33, Boston Red Sox 1934-41
*Christy Mathewson, New York Giants 1900-16, Cincinnati Reds 1916

Little League World Series Champions

Since 1947, Little League Baseball, Inc. has held its national championship in Williamsport, Pennsylvania. The organization holds eight national tournaments each year for boys and girls in different age divisions for baseball and softball. The Little League division, for 11-12 year olds, is the most famous. Beginning in 2000, 16 teams from around the world compete for the title.

YEAR	LEAGUE	CITY, COUNTRY OR U.S. STATE	YEAR	LEAGUE	CITY, COUNTRY OR U.S. STATE
1947	Maynard	Williamsport, Pennsylvania	1974	Kao Ksiung	Kao Ksiung, Chinese Taipei
1948	Lock Haven	Lock Haven, Pennsylvania	1975	Lakewood	Lakewood, New Jersey
1949	Little Big League	Hammonton, New Jersey	1976	Chofu	Tokyo, Japan
1950	National	Houston, Texas	1977	Li-The	Li-The, Chinese Taipei
1951	Stamford	Stamford, Connecticut	1978	Pin-Kuang	Pin-Kuang, Chinese Taipei
1952	National	Norwalk, Connecticut	1979	Pu-Tzu Town	Pu-Tzu Town, Chinese Taipei
1953	Southside	Birmingham, Alabama	1980	Hua Lian	Hua Lian, Chinese Taipei
1954	National	Schenectady, New York	1981	Tai-Ping	Tai-Ping, Chinese Taipei
1955	Morrisville	Morrisville, Pennsylvania	1982	Kirkland National	Kirkland, Washington
1956	Hondo Lions	Roswell, New Mexico	1983	East Marietta National	Marietta, Georgia
1957	Industrial	Monterrey, Mexico	1984	Seoul	Seoul, South Korea
1958	Industrial	Monterrey, Mexico	1985	Seoul	Seoul, South Korea
1959	National	Hamtramck, Michigan	1986	Tainan Park	Tainan Park, Chinese Taipei
1960	American	Levittown, Pennsylvania	1987	Hua Lian	Hua Lian, Chinese Taipei
1961	Northern	El Cajon/La Mesa, California	1988	Tai Chung	Tai Chung, Chinese Taipei
1962	Moreland District	San Jose, California	1989	National	Trumbull, Connecticut
1963	National	Granada Hills, California	1990	San-Hua	Chinese Taipei
1964	Mid Island	Staten Island, New York	1991	Hsi Nan	Chinese Taipei
1965	Windsor Locks	Windsor Locks, Connecticut	1992	Long Beach	Long Beach, California
1966	Westbury	Houston, Texas	1993	Long Beach	Long Beach, California
1967	West Tokyo	Tokyo, Japan	1994	Coquivacoa	Maracaibo, Venezuela
1968	Wakayama	Wakayama, Japan	1995	Shan-Hua	Shan-Hua, Chinese Taipei
1969	Taipei	Chinese Taipei	1996	Fu-Hsing	Fu-Hsing, Chinese Taipei
1970	Wayne	Wayne, New Jersey	1997	Linda Vista	Guadalupe, Mexico
1971	Tainan	Chinese Taipei	1998	Toms River East American	Toms River, New Jersey
1972	Taipei	Chinese Taipei	1999	Hirakata	Osaka, Japan
1973	Tainan	Chinese Taipei			

Glossary

AROUND THE HORN
A double play that goes from the third baseman to the second baseman to the first baseman.

ASSIST
Fielding statistic; awarded to a player who throws the ball to the fielder who makes the out.

AT-BAT
An individual batter's trip to home plate to hit. An "official" at-bat is not credited if the player walks, is hit by the pitch, sacrifices, or reaches base on catcher's interference.

BEANBALL
A pitch purposely thrown toward a batter's head. A very dangerous play and one that often provokes a violent reaction.

BLEACHERS
Seats surrounding the outfield.

BULLPEN
A separate area of a field or stadium where the relief pitchers wait their turn to enter the game. Equipped with mounds, the bullpen also is where relievers warm up their throwing arm before entering the game.

BUNT
A batted ball purposely hit into the area in front of home plate. Often used as a sacrifice to advance a runner, because the batter is usually thrown out. Some players are adept at bunting for hits by pushing the ball with the bat into an area between fielders.

CAN OF CORN
Slang term for an easy-to-catch fly ball. It comes from the way grocers used their apron to catch cans knocked from high shelves.

CATCHER'S INTERFERENCE
A rare call made when the catcher interferes with the swing of the batter (usually with his glove). The batter is awarded first base. See *Interference.*

CHANGEUP
A pitch that is thrown with the same arm motion but less speed than a fastball. Designed to keep hitters off balance.

CHOKE UP
Batting technique in which the bat is grasped several inches above the knob; it is intended to create better bat control.

CURVEBALL
A pitch thrown with a slight outward spin of the wrist at release, causing the ball to actually curve in flight. Slang terms: breaking ball, hook, Uncle Charlie.

DESIGNATED HITTER
The player who bats in the pitcher's place, but does not play a field position. In the American League, and in most college and high school leagues, pitchers do not bat. Known as the DH.

DOUBLE PLAY
Occurs when two outs are recorded on one batted ball.

DOUBLEHEADER
Two games played back-to-back. Day-night doubleheaders have a longer break between games and a separate admission often is charged.

FASTBALL
A hard, straight pitch thrown at top speed. Some pitchers make a fastball fade away from the batter or dive into a batter as it reaches the plate. Slang terms: cheese, gas, yakker.

KNUCKLE BALL
Pitch thrown with the fingertips that has an unpredictable dipping and diving motion, called knuckling. It is hard to control and harder to hit.

HIT AND RUN
Planned play in which a baserunner takes off for second base at the moment the ball is pitched; the batter's job is to hit the pitch into the hole created by the by the second baseman moving to cover the base.

HOME RUN
A hit on which the batter is able to safely touch all four bases, scoring a run. Most home runs are hit out of the playing field, but inside-the-park home runs do occur. Slang terms: circuit clout, dinger, downtown, homer, jack, round-tripper, tater.

INFIELD FLY RULE
A batter can be called out automatically by the umpire on a short fly ball that is within easy reach of an infielder in the following situation: With runners on first and second or with the bases loaded, and with less than two outs. This prevents the fielder from missing the ball on purpose and creating a double play.

INTENTIONAL WALK
Strategic move in which a player is walked on purpose to create a better situation for the defense.

INTERFERENCE
When a fielder impedes the progress of a baserunner, or when a batter or baserunner blocks the way of a fielder, interference is called by an umpire. The term is also used when a fan gets in the way of a play by reaching out or entering the playing field.

"PLAY BALL"
Traditional umpire's cry to signal the beginning of the game or restart of play after a time out.

PUTOUT
Fielding statistic; awarded to a player who tags a baserunner out or who touches a base to record an out.

RHUBARB
Slang term for an argument, usually between a manager and an umpire.

ROTATION
The order in which a manager fields his starting pitchers over the course of the season.

SACRIFICE
When a batter purposely makes an out in order to to advance a baserunner. This can be done with a bunt or with a fly ball (called a sacrifice fly).

SCREWBALL
Pitch thrown with an inward twist of the wrist and forearm at delivery, causing a sideways spin or curve of the ball. Slang term: scroogie.

SINKER
A hard, straight pitch thrown fast that drops suddenly as it reaches the plate.

SLIDER
A pitch that breaks less sharply than a curveball; thrown by rolling the ball out of the hand with less forceful action than the curveball motion.

SNOWCONE
A slang term for a catch in which the ball is partially visible above the webbing of the glove.

SOUTHPAW
A slang term for a lefthanded player, usually used for pitchers. May have derived from the fact that early parks were laid out with home plate to the west, to keep the sun out of the batter's eyes. Thus, lefthanders were pitching from the south.

TAG UP
The baserunner may not advance on a fly ball until the ball is in the fielder's mitt. To ensure that they don't leave the base too early, they tag up, or touch the base, as the fielder catches the ball.

TIME OUT
Any player can request a short break from the umpire, who holds his hands up to stop play. The ball is dead when "time" is called.

TRIPLE PLAY
When three outs are recorded on one batted ball. An unassisted triple play, when one fielder records all three outs by himself, is one of the rarest feats in baseball.

Index

Acknowledgments

Dorling Kindersley and the Shoreline Publishing Group thank the following for their invaluable assistance in creating this book: Major League Baseball Photos (Rich Pilling, Paul Cunningham); the Baseball Hall of Fame (Bill Burdick); Wilson Sporting Goods (Molly Murphy); Rawlings Sporting Goods Co. (Liz Daws); and artist George Cheney. Special thanks to coach Bill Pintard of the Santa Barbara Foresters for his pitching wisdom; to NCAA umpire Al Williams for posing so patiently; and to editor Beth Adelman for filling the author's e-mail box with fascinating baseball facts.

Picture Credits:
Pages 6-7: Old bat and old baseball, David Spindel; woodcut of children playing, Baseball Hall of Fame with colorization by Slim Films; Alexander Cartwright, A.G. Spalding, and town ball players, Baseball Hall of Fame.
Pages 8-9: Pedro Martinez of the Boston Red Sox on pitching mound, Sam Smith/MLB Photos; diamond and batters' boxes illustrations, George Cheney; 1888 diamond, Baseball Hall of Fame; foul pole, Mike Eliason; home plate, Dorling Kindersley.
Pages 10-11: Babe Ruth swings, Baseball Hall of Fame; Jim Thome of the Cleveland Indians scores a run and Chuck Knoblauch of the New York Yankees out at first, AP/Wide World; strike zone diagram, George Cheney; Alex Rodriguez of the Seattle Mariners makes a tag, Brad Mangin/MLB Photos; Larry Walker of the Colorado Rockies catches a fly ball, Bob Rosato/MLB Photos.
Pages 12-13: Babe Ruth autographed baseball, David Spindel; interior and exterior of baseballs, courtesy Rawlings Sporting Goods; bat construction steps and Louisville Slugger bat, Michael Burr; Ruth and Maris bats, AP/Wide World.
Pages 14-15: Fingerless glove, Baseball Hall of Fame; old glove and Gold Glove trophy, David Spindel; fielder's, first baseman's, and pitcher's gloves, courtesy Wilson Sporting Goods; batting glove, courtesy Franklin Sports; Mark McGwire of the St. Louis Cardinals at first base, MLB Photos.
Pages 16-17: Old-time uniform, Baseball Hall of Fame; Babe Ruth and Lou Gehrig, AP/Wide World; batting helmet, courtesy Rawlings Sporting Goods; baseball spikes courtesy Nike; cap and all uniform photos, Al Messerschmidt.
Pages 18-19: Mickey Cochrane, AP/Wide World; modern catcher's mask, catcher's helmet, modern catcher's mitts, courtesy Rawlings Sporting Goods; hockey-style mask, MLB Photos; old-time mask and mitt, David Spindel; catcher in gear, Michael Burr.

Pages 20-21: Pitcher Randy Johnson of the Arizona Diamondbacks, AP/Wide World; catcher Charles Johnson of the Baltimore Orioles, Mitchell Layton/MLB Photos; first baseman Jeff Bagwell of the Houston Astros, second baseman Roberto Alomar of the Cleveland Indians, shortstop Rey Ordonez of the New York Mets, Rich Pilling/MLB Photos; third baseman Matt Williams of the Arizona Diamondbacks, left fielder Barry Bonds of the San Francisco Giants, Brad Mangin/MLB Photos; center fielder Andruw Jones of the Atlanta Braves, Allen Kee/MLB Photos; right fielder Tony Gwynn of the San Diego Padres, Joel Zwink/MLB Photos.
Pages 22-23: Bernie Williams of the New York Yankees catches a fly ball, MLB Photos; Mike Piazza of the New York Mets chases a foul pop, Larry Walker of the Colorado Rockies throws the ball, Bob Rosato/MLB Photos; Ivan Rodriguez of the Texas Rangers blocks the plate, Brad Mangin/MLB Photos; catcher receives, Michael Burr; Nomar Garciaparra of the Boston Red Sox throws, Derek Jeter of the New York Yankees fields a grounder, Rich Pilling/MLB Photos; double play and cutoff diagrams, George Cheney.
Pages 24-25: Derek Jeter of the New York Yankees, Bob Rosato/MLB Photos; pine tar rag, shin guard, Al Messerschmidt; batting sequence, Michael Burr; strike zone, release point, hit chart illustrations, George Cheney; Stan Musial, Mel Ott, Rod Carew, AP/Wide World.
Pages 26-27: Pitching grips, catcher's signs, Michael Burr; Andy Ashby of the Philadelphia Phillies in pitch sequence, pitcher with rosin bag, Al Messerschmidt; Dennis Eckersley, AP/Wide World; home plate and side view diagrams, George Cheney.
Pages 28-29: Bases (2), foot on base, Al Messerschmidt; Paul O'Neill of the New York Yankees slides into second, Rich Pilling/MLB Photos; Rickey Henderson of the New York Mets slides, AP/Wide World; running bases and stolen base diagrams, George Cheney.
Pages 30-31: Managers meet at home plate, AP/Wide World; coach flashes signs (5), Al Messerschmidt; Baltimore Orioles lineup card from the first game Cal Ripken Jr. missed after 2,632 consecutive games, AP/Wide World.
Pages 32-33: Old-time umpire, Baseball Hall of Fame; brush, David Spindel; indicator, Michael Burr; umpire position diagram, George Cheney; home plate umpire and umpire signals (8), Russ McConnell.
Pages 34-35: Fenway Park, Steve Babineau/MLB Photos; Wrigley Field, Steve Green/MLB Photos; old-time stadium, Baseball Hall of Fame; Turner Field, Al Messerschmidt; Ebbets Field, AP/Wide World; Skydome, Bob Rosato; Cinergy Field, Joe Giblich/MLB Photos; Pacific Bell Park drawing courtesy San Francisco Giants/HOK.
Pages 36-37: Announcer in booth, Cal Ripken waves at Camden Yards, AP/Wide World; Wrigley Field scoreboard, Ron Vesely/MLB Photos; Henry Chadwick, Baseball Hall of Fame; 1888 scorecard, Library of Congress.

Pages 38-39: Total Baseball cover, courtesy Total Sports; printed statistics and standings, courtesy MLB Properties.
Pages 44-45: Don Larsen hugs Yogi Berra, AP/Wide World; 1903 World Series program, 1954 World Series ring, David Spindel; 1999 World Series program, courtesy Major League Baseball Properties; 1994 World Series baseball, Michael Burr; Commissioner's Trophy, MLB Photos; Scott Brosius of the New York Yankees with MVP trophy, Bob Rosato/MLB Photos; Livan Hernandez of the Florida Marlins, Michael Zagaris/MLB Photos; 1988 World Series ticket courtesy of David Ginsberg.
Pages 46-47: Baseball Hall of Fame exterior, interior collections cases (2), movie theater display, Jackie Robinson's hat, Joe DiMaggio's jersey, Baseball Hall of Fame; George Brett plaque, Nolan Ryan baseball and Class of 1939, AP/Wide World.
Pages 48-49: Christy Mathewson, Tris Speaker, Library of Congress; Honus Wagner card, Christie's; Jackie Robinson, David Spindel; Phil Niekro/Nolan Ryan, courtesy of Cameron Reid; Wade Boggs, Cal Ripken, Jr., baseball card pack, Larry Walker card back, courtesy of Upper Deck Company.
Pages 50-51: All-American Girls' League action, courtesy University of Notre Dame Library; Peoria pennant, Baseball Hall of Fame; Josh Gibson, Satchel Paige, LSU player Warren Morris, the Famous Chicken, minor leaguers, Ila Borders, AP/Wide World.
Pages 52-53: Young catcher, tee-ball player, Mike Eliason; Cal Ripken, Jr. teaches youngster, Little League field, Little League World Series, Japanese youngsters, AP/Wide World; youth bat, Little League World Series pins, Michael Burr; youth glove courtesy Wilson Sporting Goods.
Pages 54-55: Softball, courtesy Wilson Sporting Goods; softball fast-pitch sequence, softball slow-pitch sequence, Mike Eliason; softball batter, AP/Wide World; stickball batter, AP/Wide World; over-the-line batter, courtesy Dale Olson and the Old Mission Beach Athletic Club; over-the-line and softball field diagrams, George Cheney.
Pages 56-57: 1996 Olympic baseball action between Australia and the Netherlands, AP/Wide World; Japanese batter, Mike Piazza of the New York Mets in Japan, MLB Photos; Mexican pitcher, Cuban pitcher, Fidel Castro, AP/Wide World; world map, Slim Films; Japanese newspaper kindly provided by John Gordon.
Pages 58-59: Hank Aaron of the Atlanta Braves, Carl Yastrzemski of the Boston Red Sox, Mark McGwire of the St. Louis Cardinals, MLB Photos; David Cone of the New York Yankees, John Williamson/MLB Photos; Cal Ripken, Jr., of the Baltimore Orioles, Rich Pilling/MLB Photos.
Pages 60: Ken Griffey, Jr., of the Cincinnati Reds, Rich Pilling/MLB Photos.